AF412437

WAR IS SWELL

WAR IS SWELL

WILLIAM ANTHONY

Smart Art Press/Track 16 Gallery

Bergamot Station
2525 Michigan Avenue, Building C1
Santa Monica, California 90404
310-264-4678 (tel)
310-264-4682 (fax)
www.smartartpress.com

Smart Art Press
Volume VII, No. 67

©2000 Smart Art Press

Editor: Susan Martin
Design: William Anthony and Brains
Copy Editor: Sherri Schottlaender

Distributed by RAM Publications
2525 Michigan Avenue, Building A2
Santa Monica, California 90404
310-453-0043 (tel)
310-264-4888 (fax)
rampub@gte.net

ISBN: 1-889195-39-1
Printed in Spain at Jomagar, S.L.

FOR JONATHAN WILLIAMS

AND THOMAS MEYER

Also by William Anthony

A New Approach to Figure Drawing
1965

Bible Stories
1978

Bill Anthony's Greatest Hits
1988

SOME RANDOM THOUGHTS ABOUT *WAR IS SWELL*

William Anthony

This book tells in pictures and words a kid's-eye view of World War II. I was seven when the war started and almost eleven when it ended.

My boyhood friends and I were a lucky bunch. None of us had fathers killed or wounded. The war was something that happened in letters from overseas and in reports on the radio and in newspapers, and in the comics.

We loved the fighting men and combat. We loved the air raids and the commando raids and the plots to kill Hitler. We loved the action behind the lines, under the seas, and in the prisoner-of-war camps. We loved the heroics of the Allies and the villainy of the enemy. We were enthusiastic scholars of the tortures practiced by the Axis.

*   *   *   *

It never occurred to me that we could lose the war. In fact, I could hardly conceive of our losing a battle. On D-Day I remember that I couldn't understand my parents' concern that the Allies might be thrown back into the Channel. I had no doubt that we would triumph at the Battle of the Bulge and on every Pacific island.

I'm sure my vision of the war will seem totally incomprehensible to anyone who was not an American kid in the 1940s. A tale told by a grossly misinformed idiot. But still, for me, this is an accurate account of how I remember the war.

*   *   *   *

The language of an eleven-year-old in 1945 was not tempered by political correctness. It's unfortunate that the words "Jap" and "Kraut" are part of the vocabulary here; however, a more polite word like "Japanese" was hardly in use at the time.

At first I tried putting quotation marks around offensive words, but it didn't work. Quotation marks around every offensive sentence were even less successful.

In the initial printing of *The Naked and the Dead*, Norman Mailer had to substitute "fug" for "fuck." I remember reading the novel when I was a teenager and thinking that since the war, the pronunciation of the word had actually changed. I'm not anxious to commit this sort of revisionism.

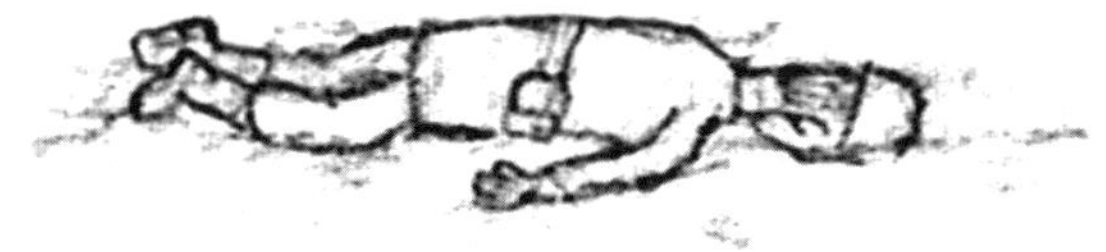

My drawing style is derived from the mistakes of my students. The following excerpt is from an interview with me that appeared in *The Paris Review* (Spring 1976 issue).

INTERVIEWER: How did you arrive at this style of drawing?

ANTHONY: A number of years ago when I was on the West Coast, I taught drawing at a commercial art school. My students wanted to learn to draw accurately, that is, to draw a hand that looked like a hand. To help them I did exaggerations of the mistakes which beginners make: heads too large, torsos like sandbags, skinny necks, legs resembling carrots, elbows and knees that looked as though they'd suffered from some sort of tourniquet treatment. I put all these mistakes together to form a classically idiotic figure. Then this satiric how-not-to took on an insane life of its own in my work.

The eleven-year-old makes essentially the same mistakes as an adult; however, unlike the adult, he is not hindered by any great desire to correct his blunders. At age eleven I had no concern with the fact that my draftsmanship displayed "heads too large, torsos like sandbags, skinny necks and legs resembling carrots." It was full steam ahead in portraying the bravery of the Allies and the evil of the enemy; don't confuse me with anatomical facts.

The mindlessness of the style underscores the simplicity of my view of the war: Us against the bad guys.

The fact that my style is distilled from kids' drawing blunders compels me to do a lot of kid subject matter. Besides war, I do cowboys and Indians, scenes of crime and punishment, and man versus beast.

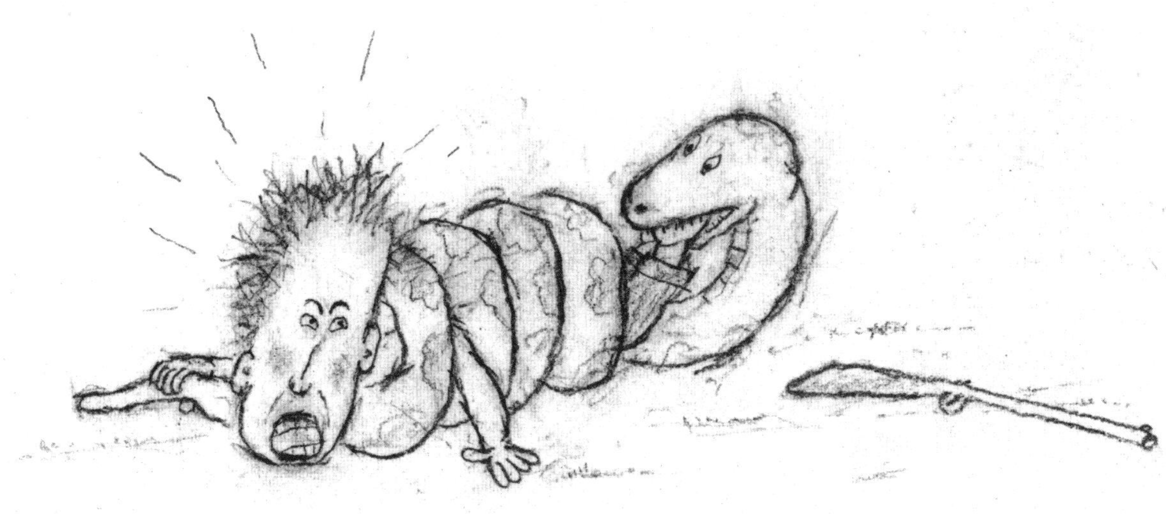

The list continues with a boy's skewed version of great historic events (e.g., Robespierre dragged kicking and screaming to the guillotine) to an eleven-year-old's prurient idea of the sexual proclivities of his elders (e.g., a panoramic view of a police raid on a whorehouse).

I hoped to start my military adventures by spotting enemy planes near our home in a suburb of Tacoma, Washington. I fantasized about phoning the nearby army air base, McCord Field.

"Hi, McCord Field? This is Billy Anthony reporting. There are seven Jap Zeroes, three Jap Bettys, and two Kraut Dornier-17s over my house, going east."

"OK, Billy, we'll send some P-38s right over to shoot 'em down. By the way, thanks for collecting all that scrap paper and metal for the war effort. We make P-38s out of scrap aluminum."

"You're sure welcome!"

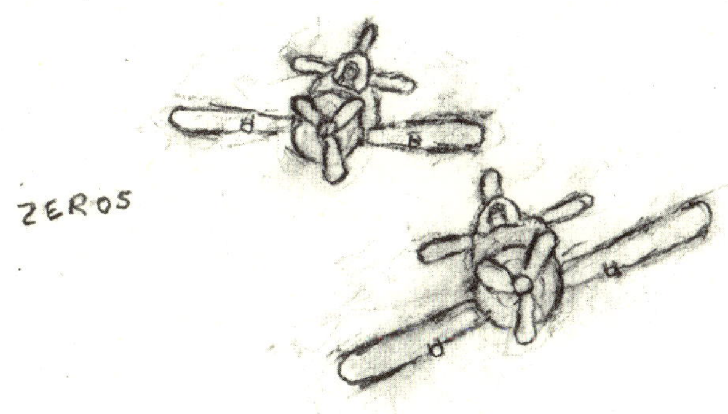

Like the stars who volunteered to entertain the troops and the natives who helped our downed fliers, if I couldn't get in on the fighting, at least I could help.

Early in the war (I was probably eight), I had the vague idea that warplanes had souls, or something akin to souls. Stukas and Zeroes were always committing horrendous deeds, seeming to operate with pilotless minds of their own.

The most likely candidate for soulhood was the Stuka. A mere machine couldn't exude such nifty malevolence.

On the other hand, I never felt that tanks had souls, not even Rommel's tanks. I knew a tank was something like a car, only it had armor and treads.

I wasn't visually sophisticated enough to distinguish between the Allied and Axis tanks. As far as I was concerned, they could all be represented by a potato-like lump on top of another larger potato-like lump. Add gun barrel to top lump and treads to bottom lump.

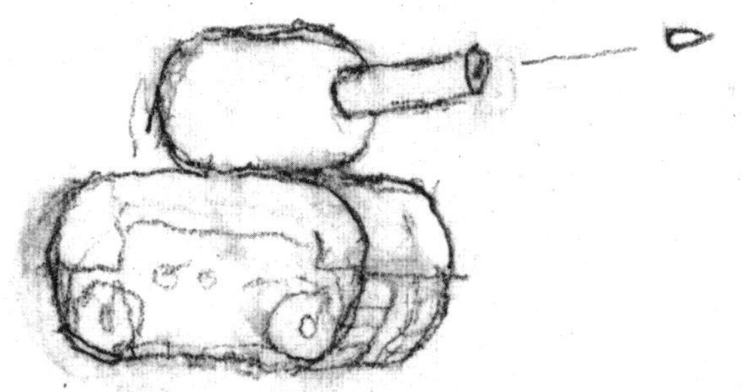

Included in the book are some curious events that would have appealed to any boy draftsman at the time of the war. Some are actually true.

Hitler had a riding crop made of hippopotamus hide. Admiral Yamamoto did put tacks on the chairs of his subordinate officers. The wheels were in fact rigged to come off some kamikaze planes at takeoff (although I never read of a kamikaze pilot being manhandled in the cockpit of his plane). General Keitel did have his staff officers sing for Hitler.

General Patton did swear that he would pee in the Rhine River; I don't know that he did it. Eva Braun owned forbidden jazz records, but it is not established that she boogied to them.

On the other hand, Hitler didn't dance in jubilation at the conquest of France or any other country. Early in the war the Allies' propaganda mill artfully doctored some film that made it appear that Hitler was doing a jig at the French surrender at Compiègne. As Picasso remarked, "Art is a lie that makes us realize the truth."

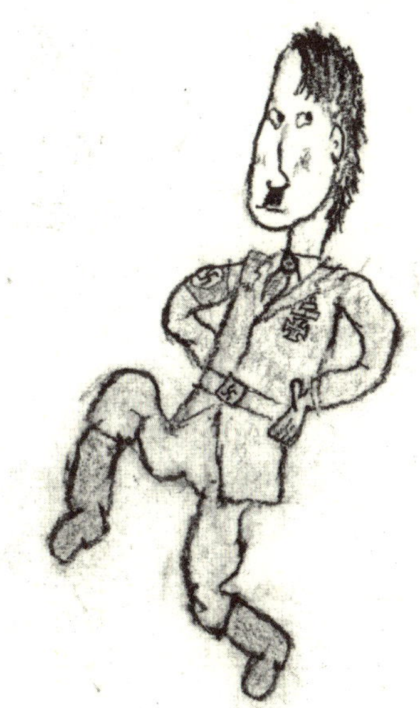

The large two-page naval-air battle (a few pages after Pearl Harbor) includes a German plane among the Japanese dive bombers attacking one of the American battleships (upper right corner). I call this "an exchange Stuka," strictly something I made up.

*   *   *   *

The main purpose of World War II was to catch and punish Hitler and Tojo. If you had asked me, I would have said they should be dipped in shit. Both of 'em. I'd help.

*   *   *   *

If you want to know why the world has been so productive of "ignorant armies [that] clash by night," read on. I feel that the worldview of this hare-brained, home-front Herodotus (me), though simplistic, racist, and inaccurate, explains much.

The Japs, they started it by
bombing Pearl Harbor.

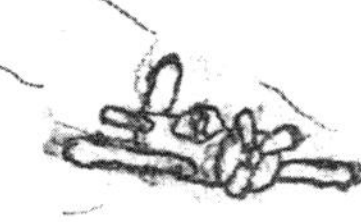

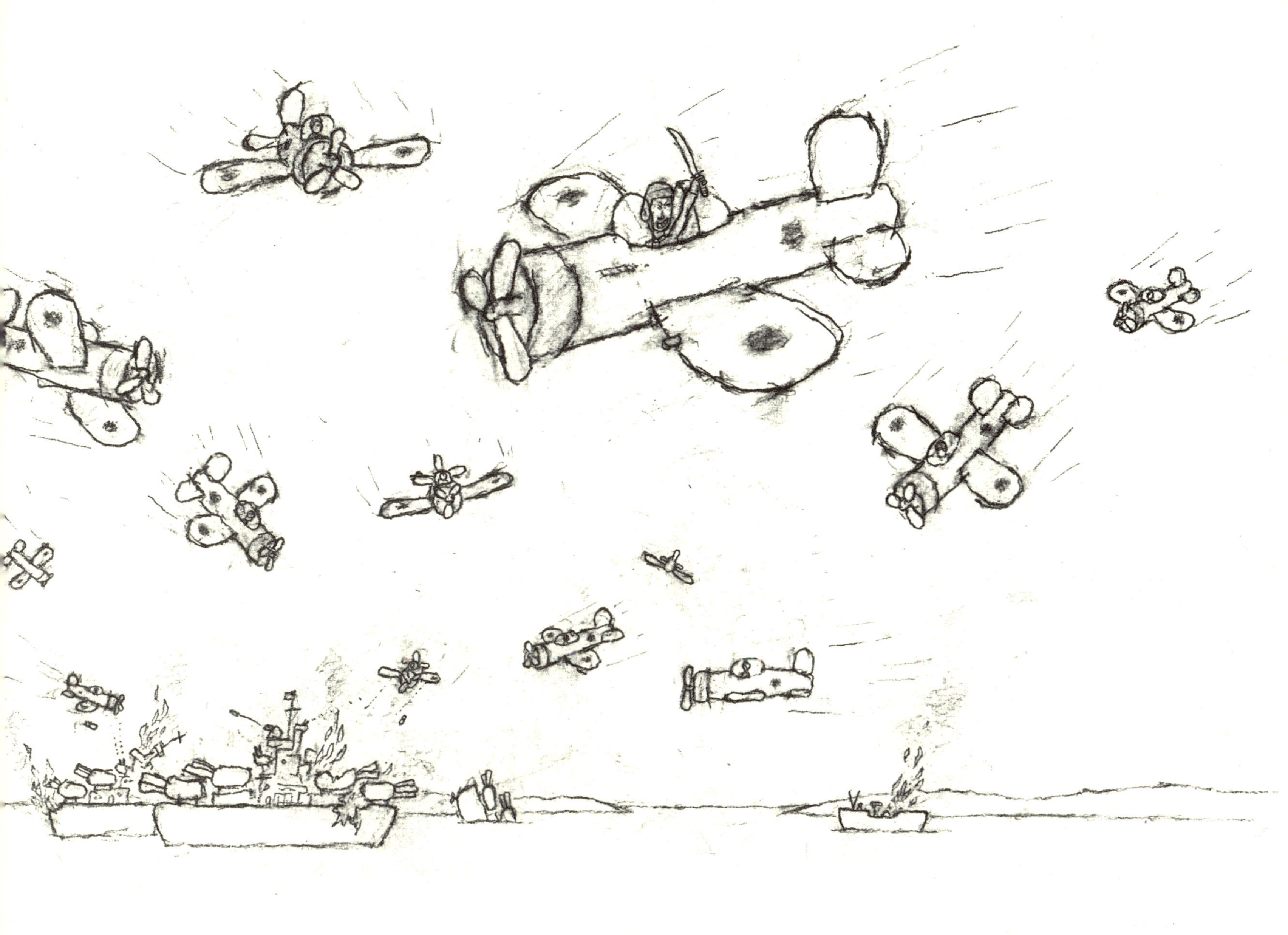

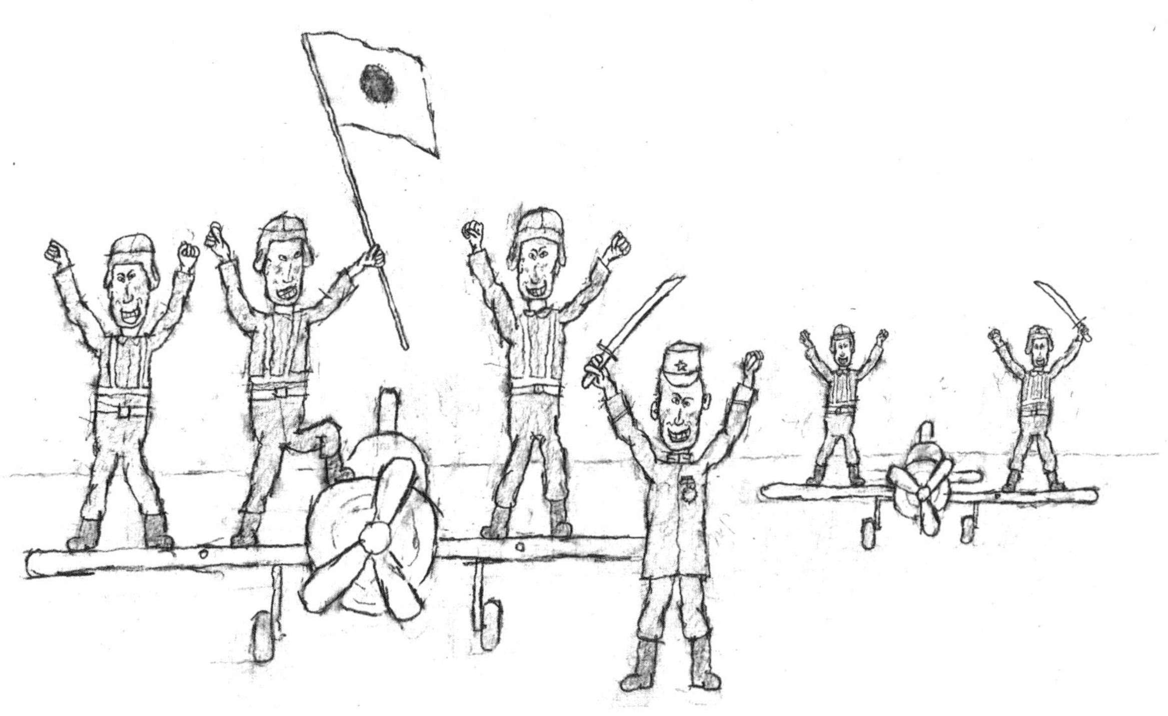

After their sneaky attack the little
nippers stood around waving their
meatball flag and getting photographed.

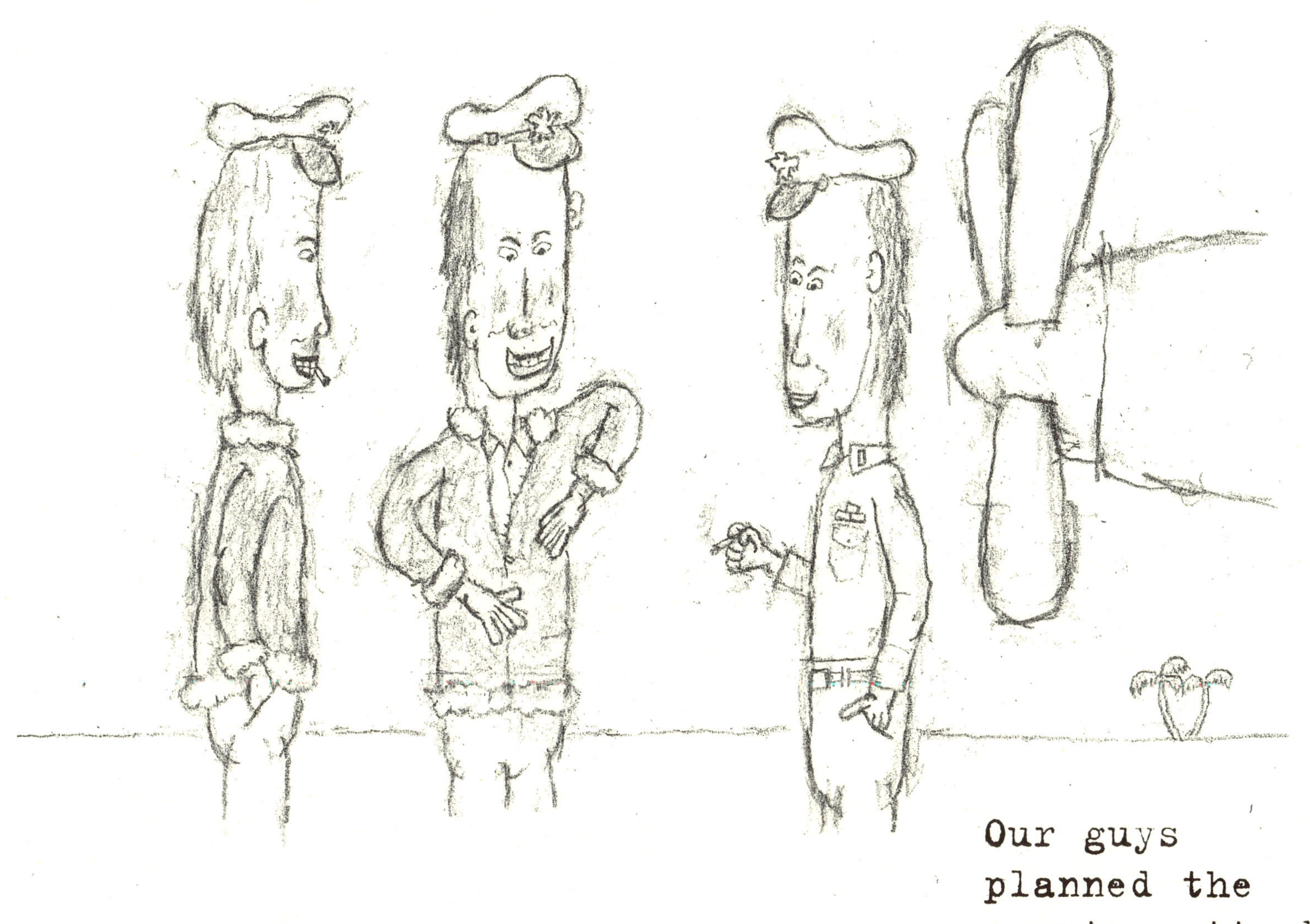

Our guys
planned the
counter-attack.

REVENGE

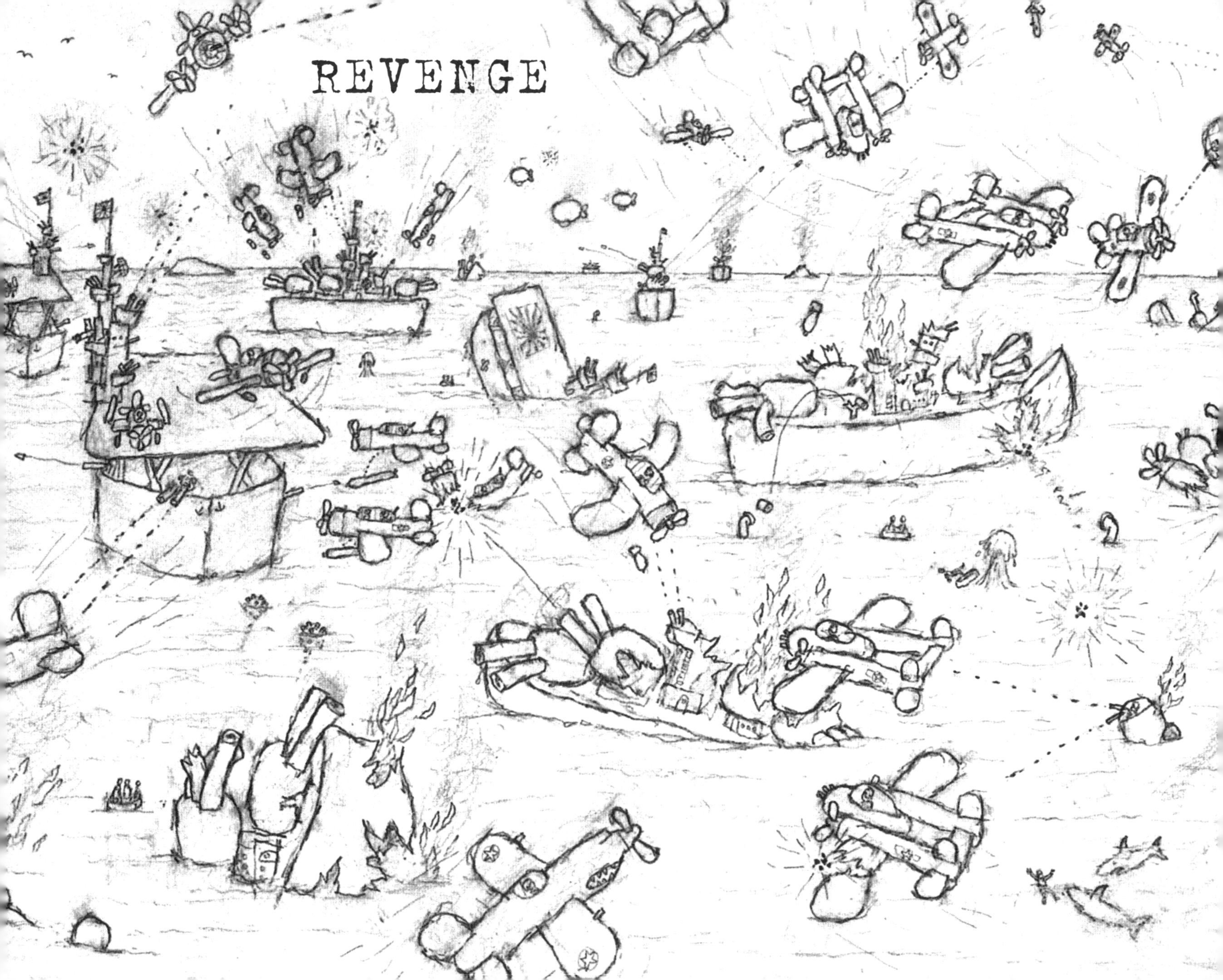

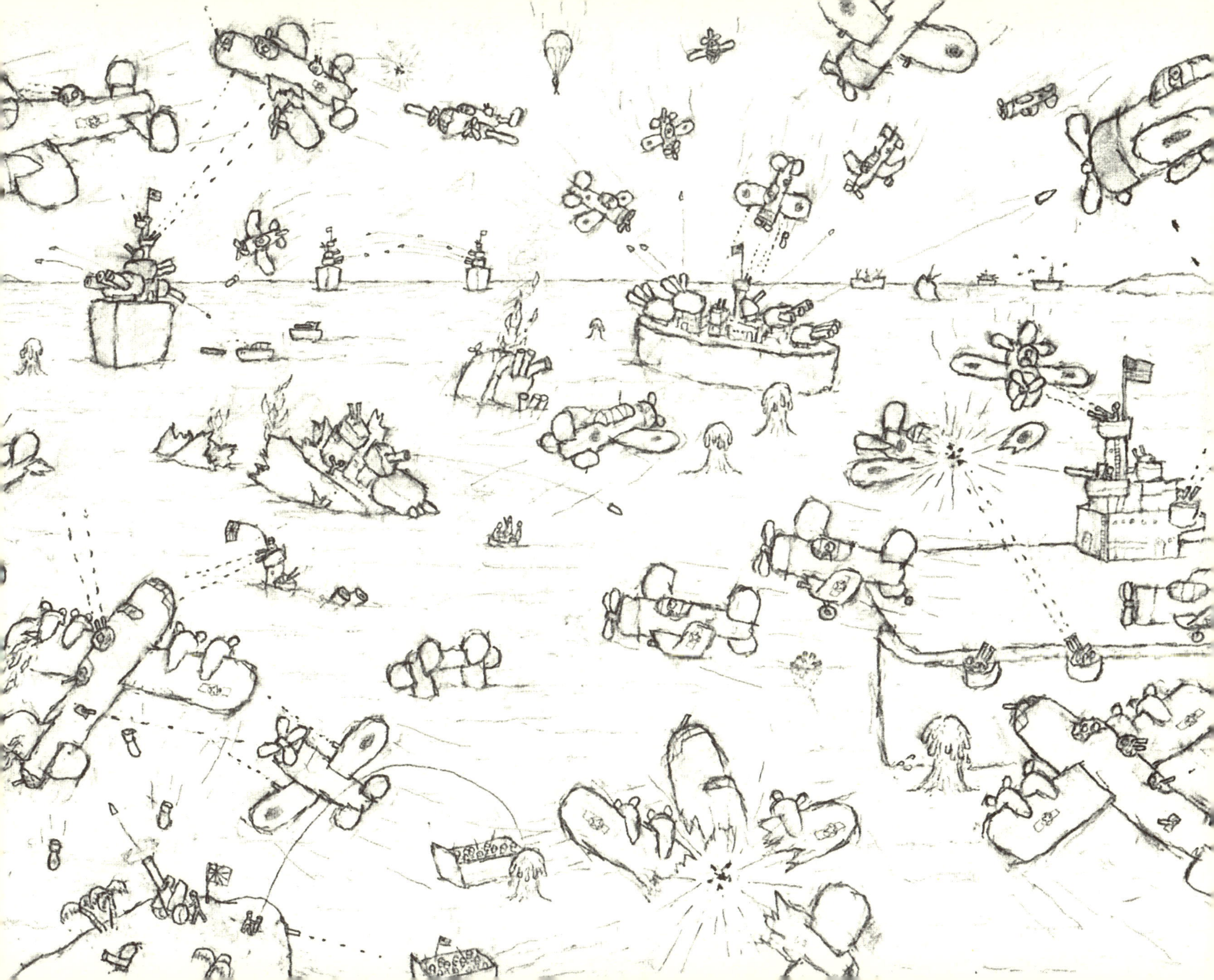

After every battle a lot of our guys
were left on lifeboats and ran out
of water.

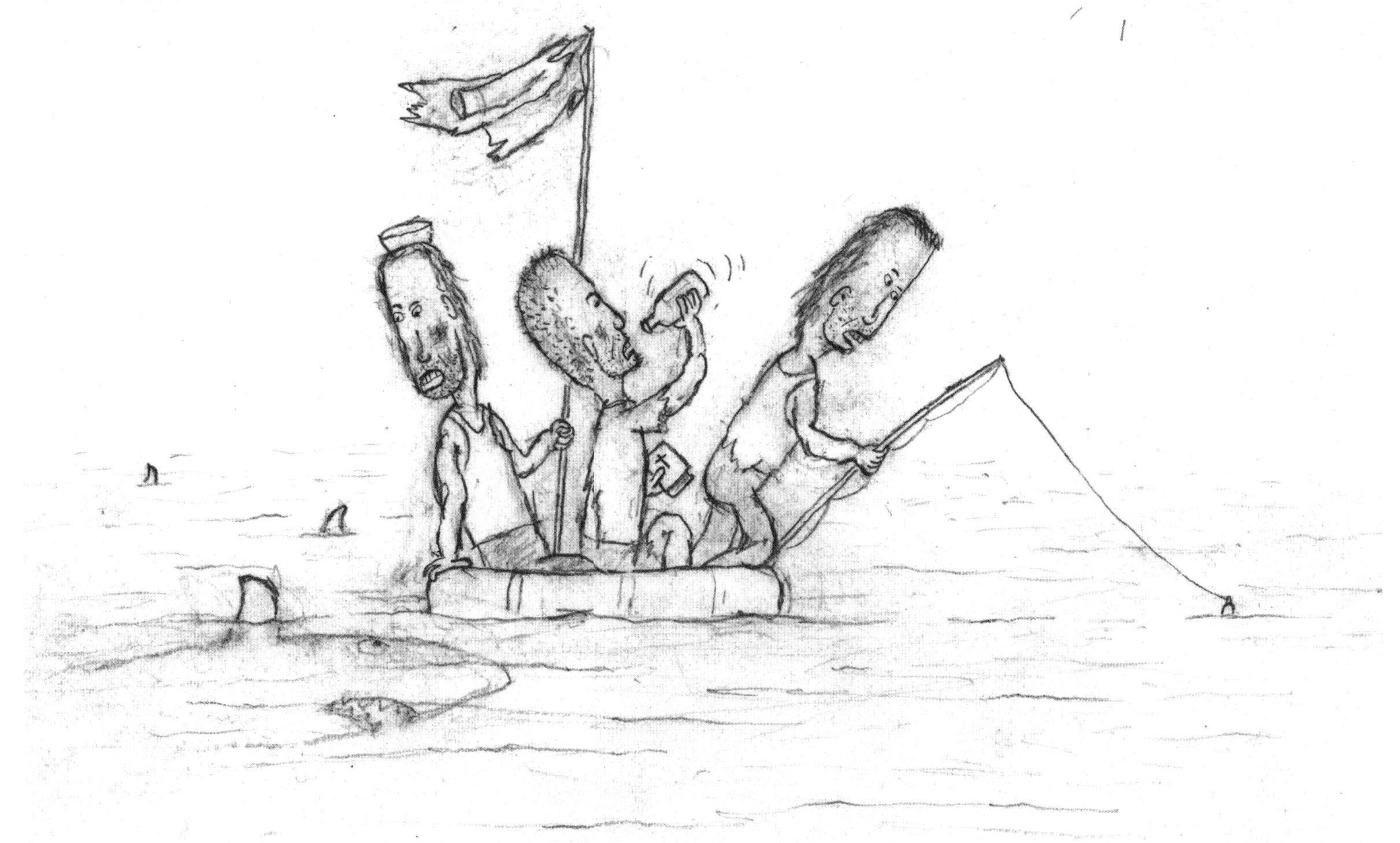

Admiral Yamamoto was in charge of the Jap
navy. He liked to put tacks on the chairs
used by the other officers, just to make
sure they would stay alert.

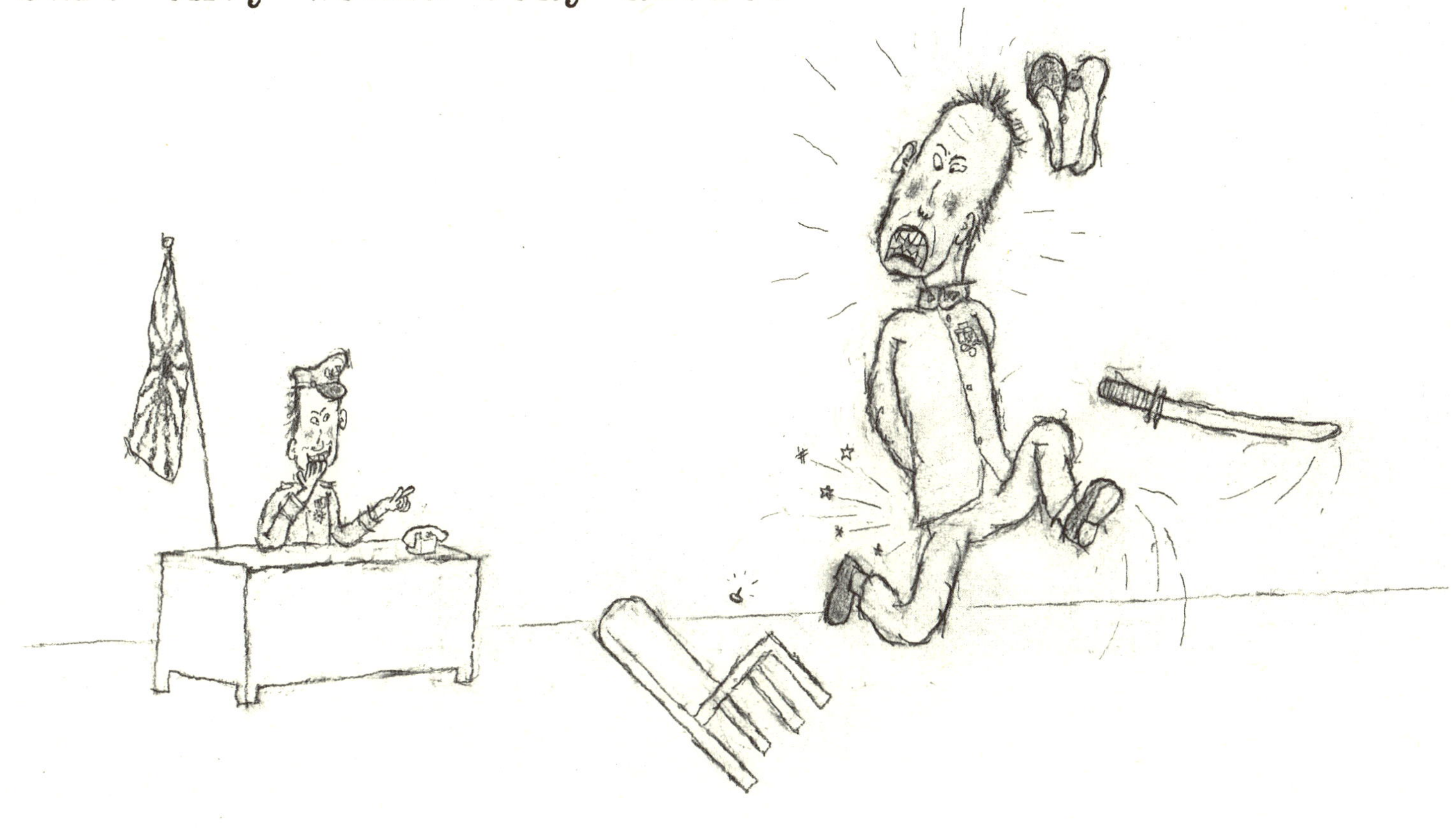

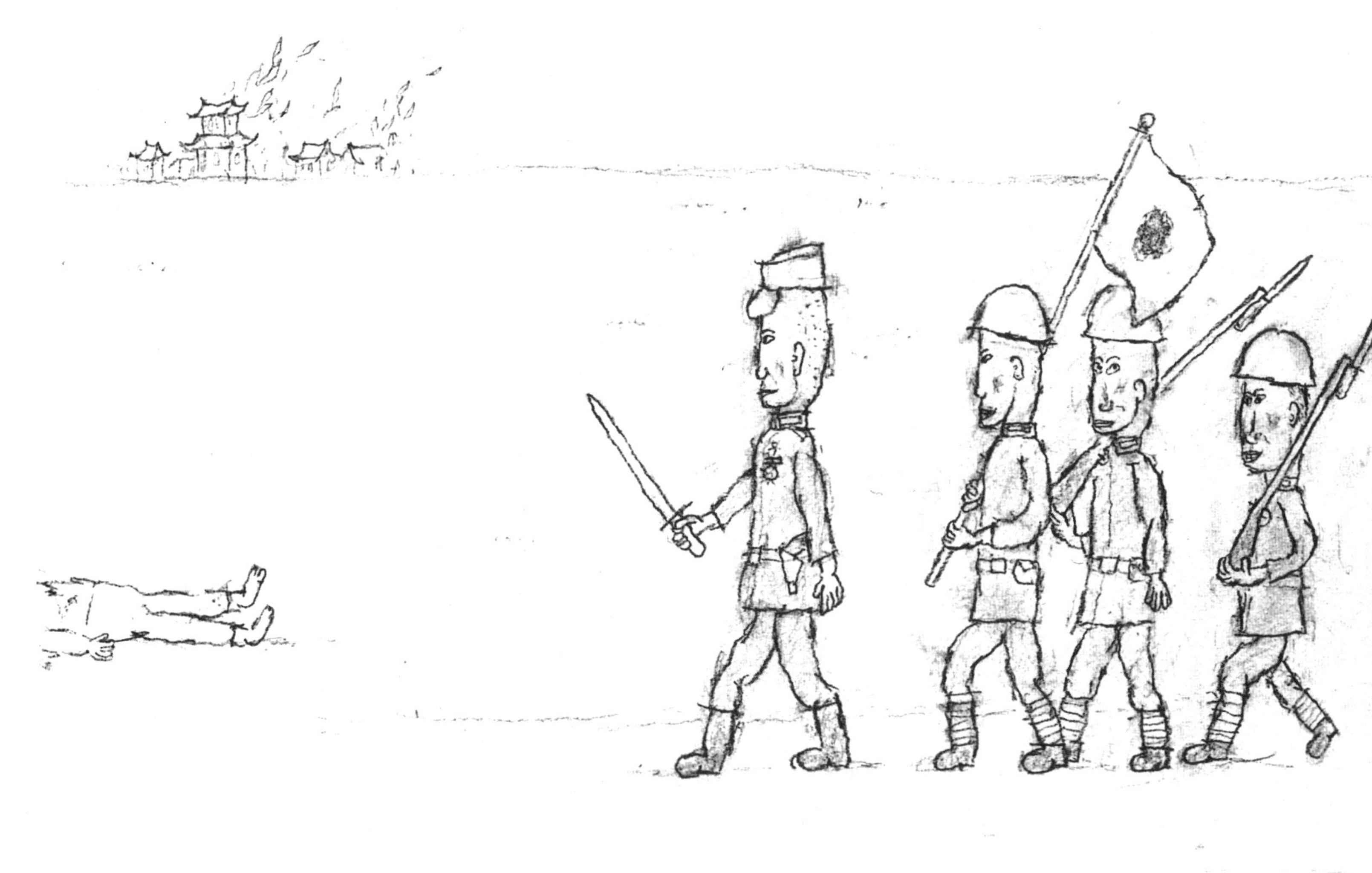

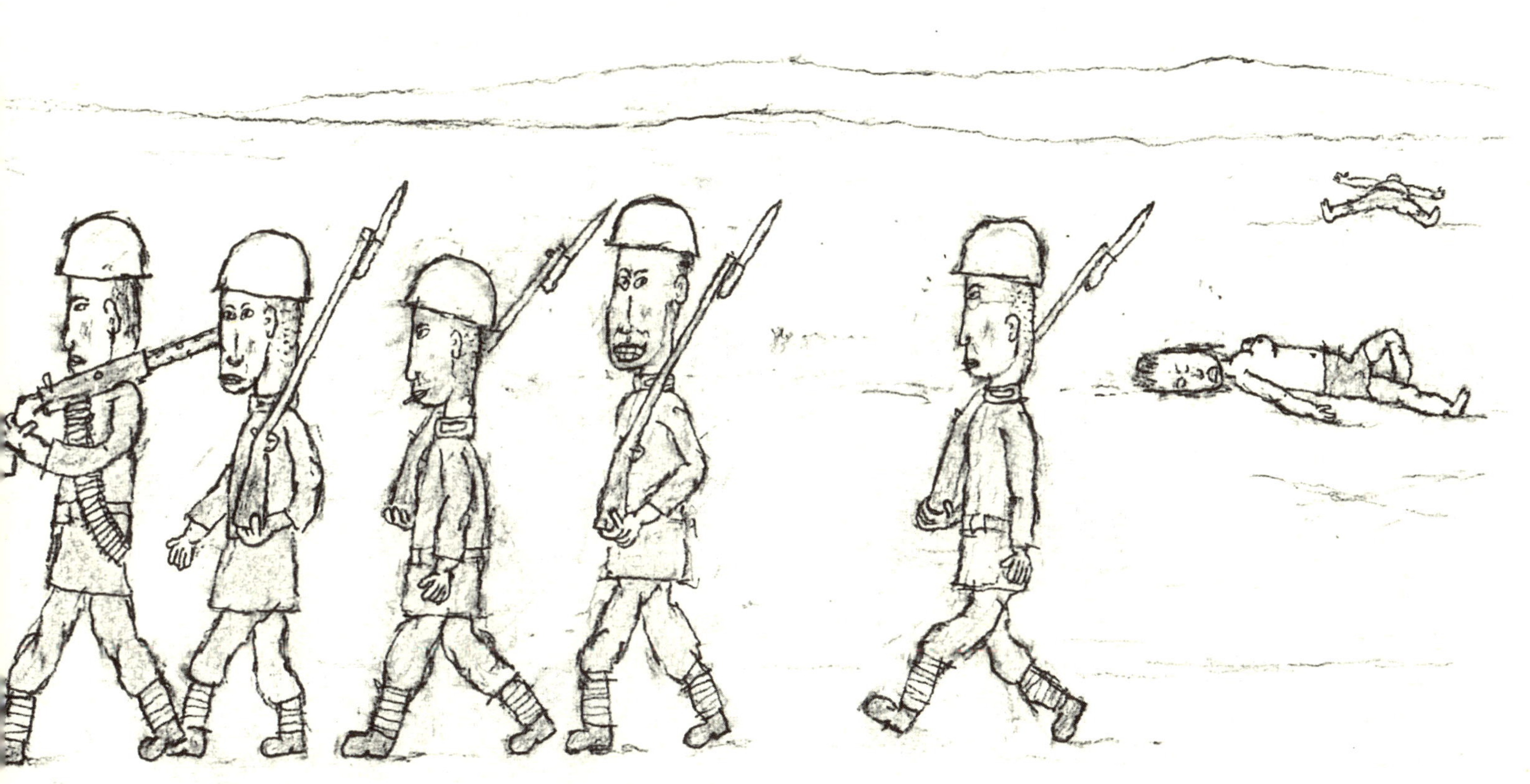

The Japs were always invading China.
They usually won 'cause they fought dirty.

In Japan everyone had to bow
down to Tojo, the head Jap.

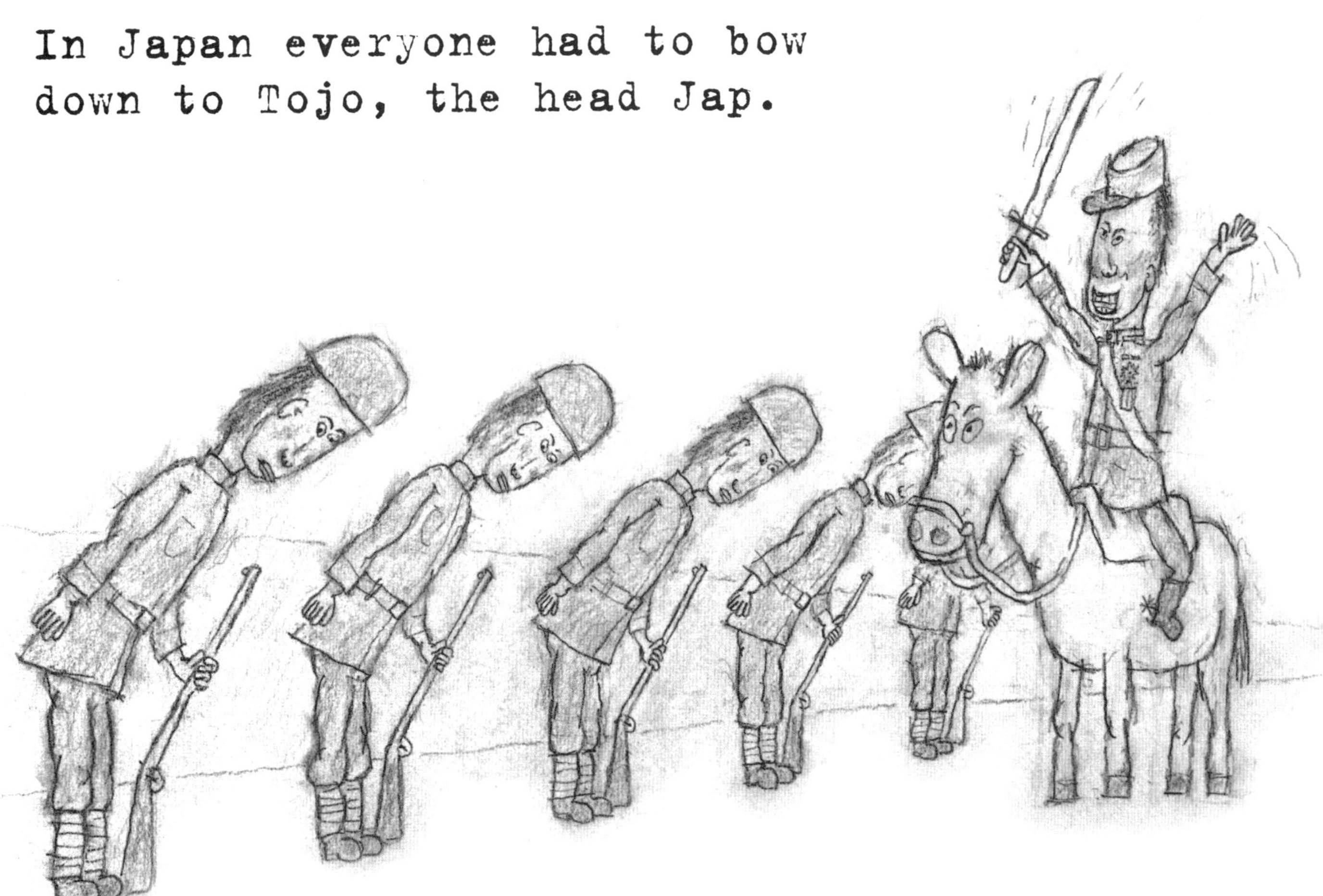

Then Germany started acting up.

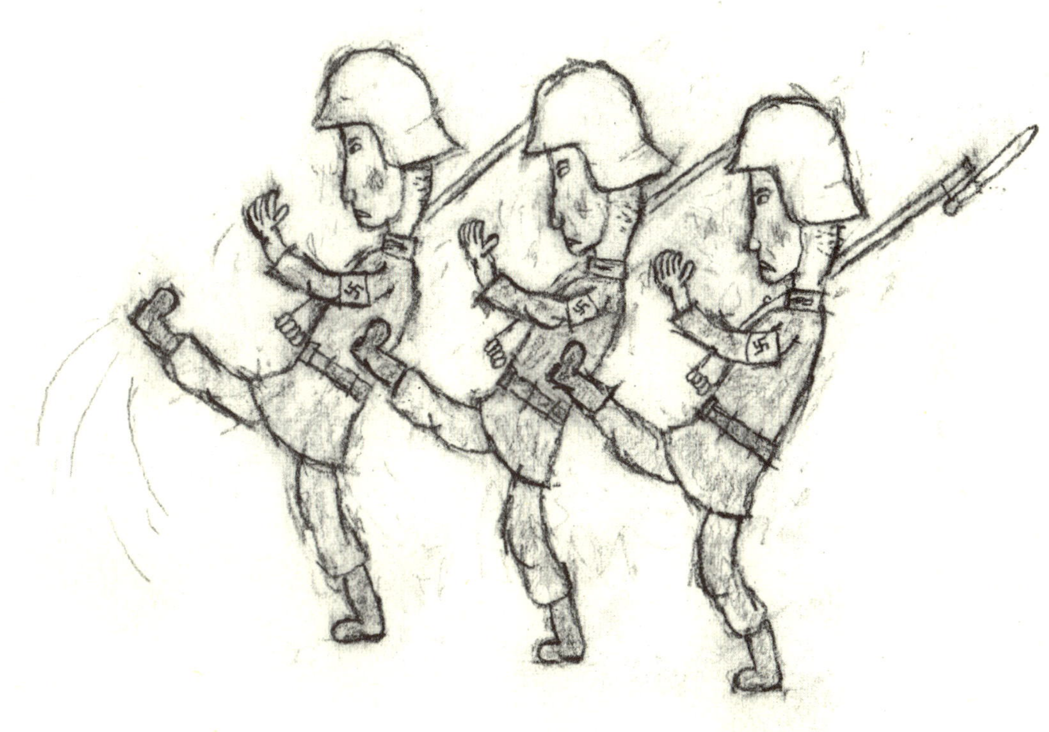

Hitler was a
paperhanger who got
this job as dictator
of Germany.
He spent most of his
time having tantrums.

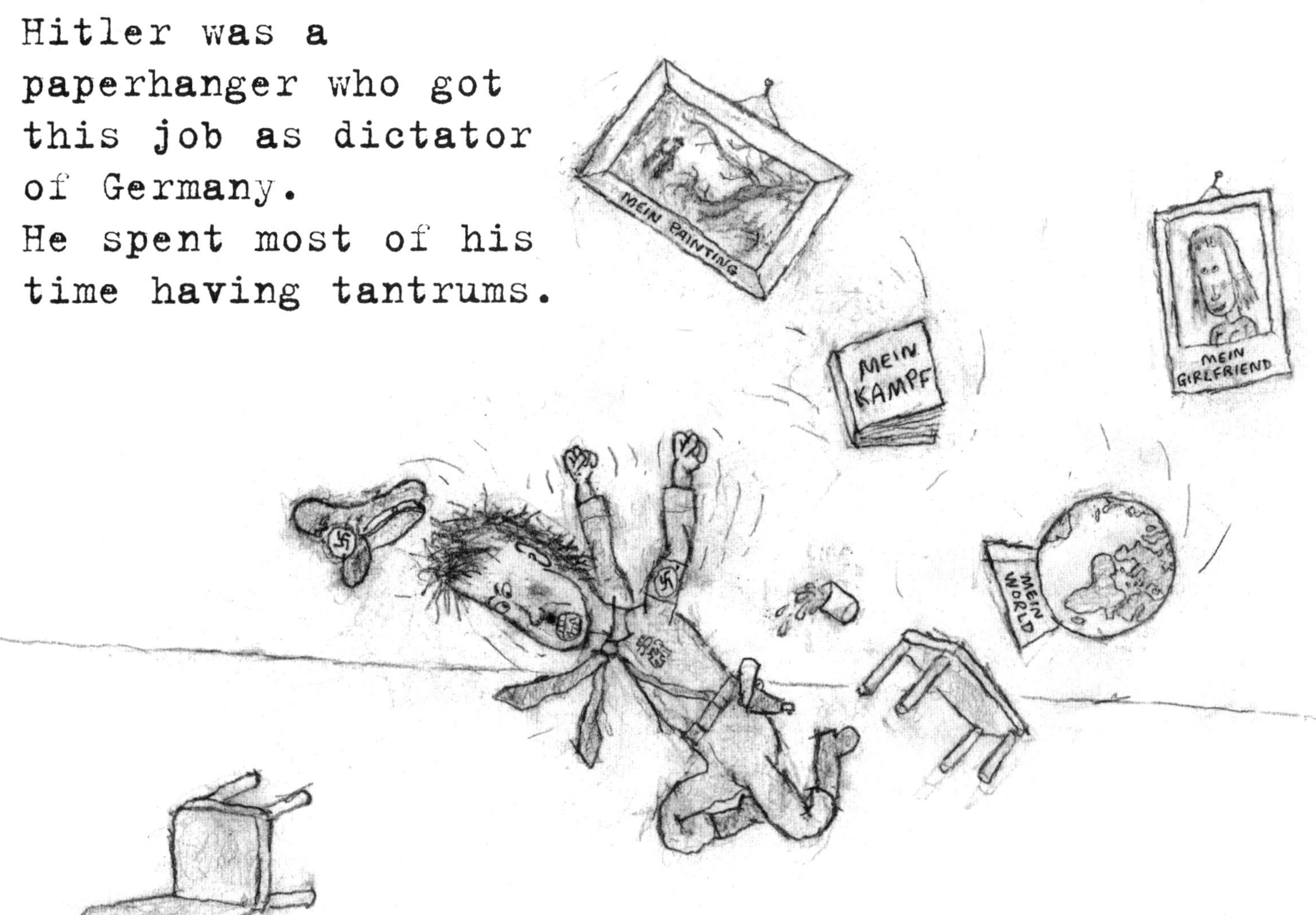

Hitler always carried a
riding crop made out of
genuine hippopotamus hide.

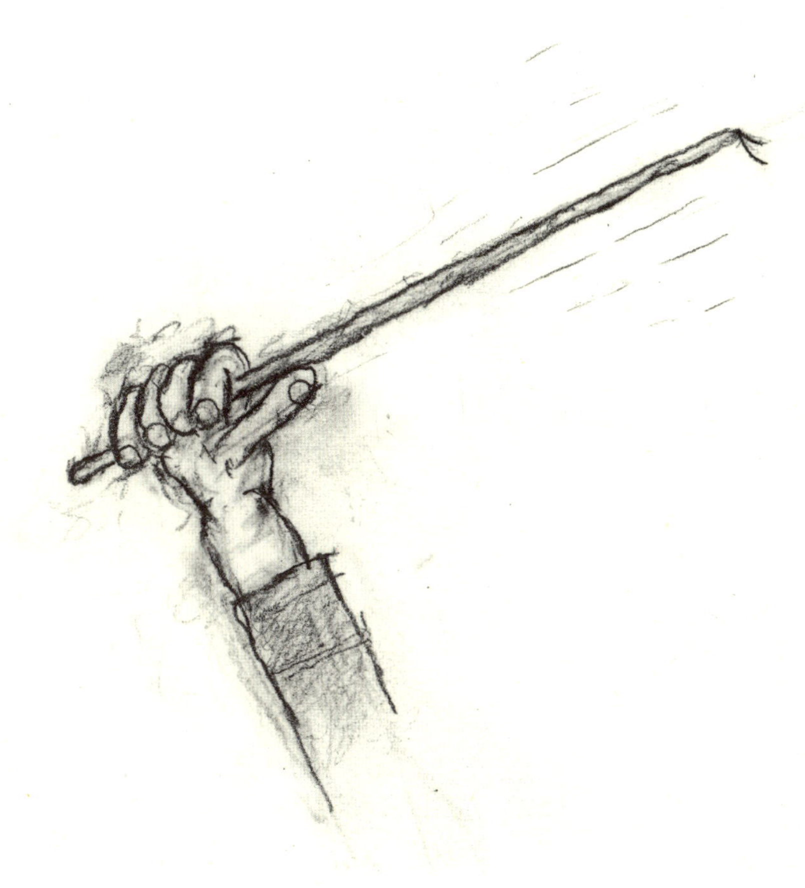

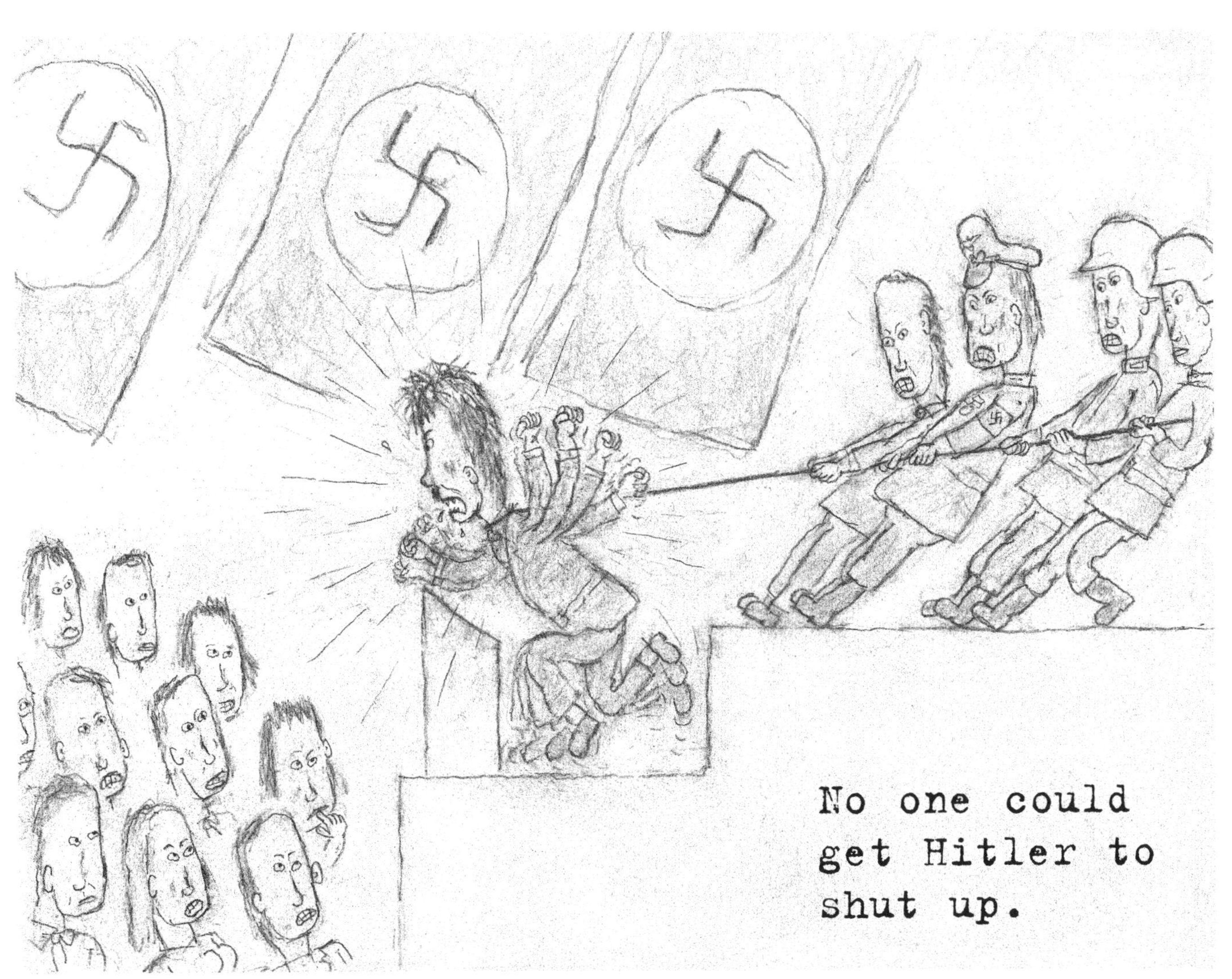

No one could
get Hitler to
shut up.

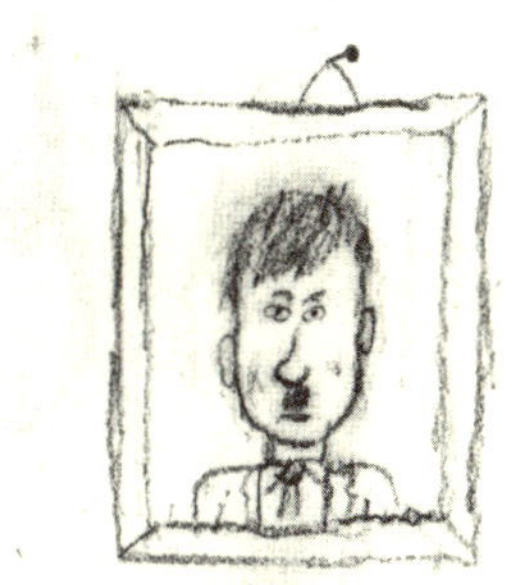

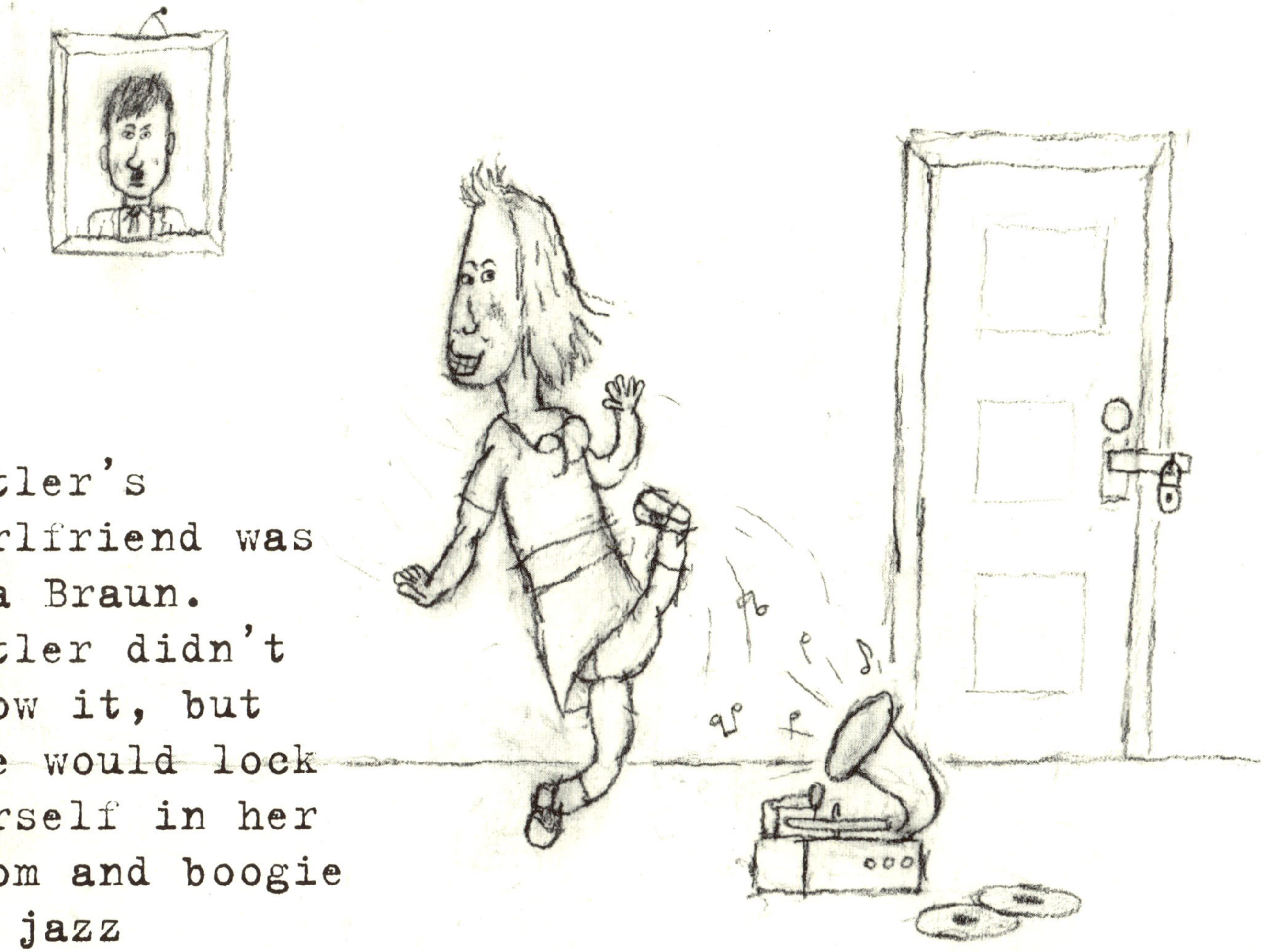

Hitler's
girlfriend was
Eva Braun.
Hitler didn't
know it, but
she would lock
herself in her
room and boogie
to jazz
records.

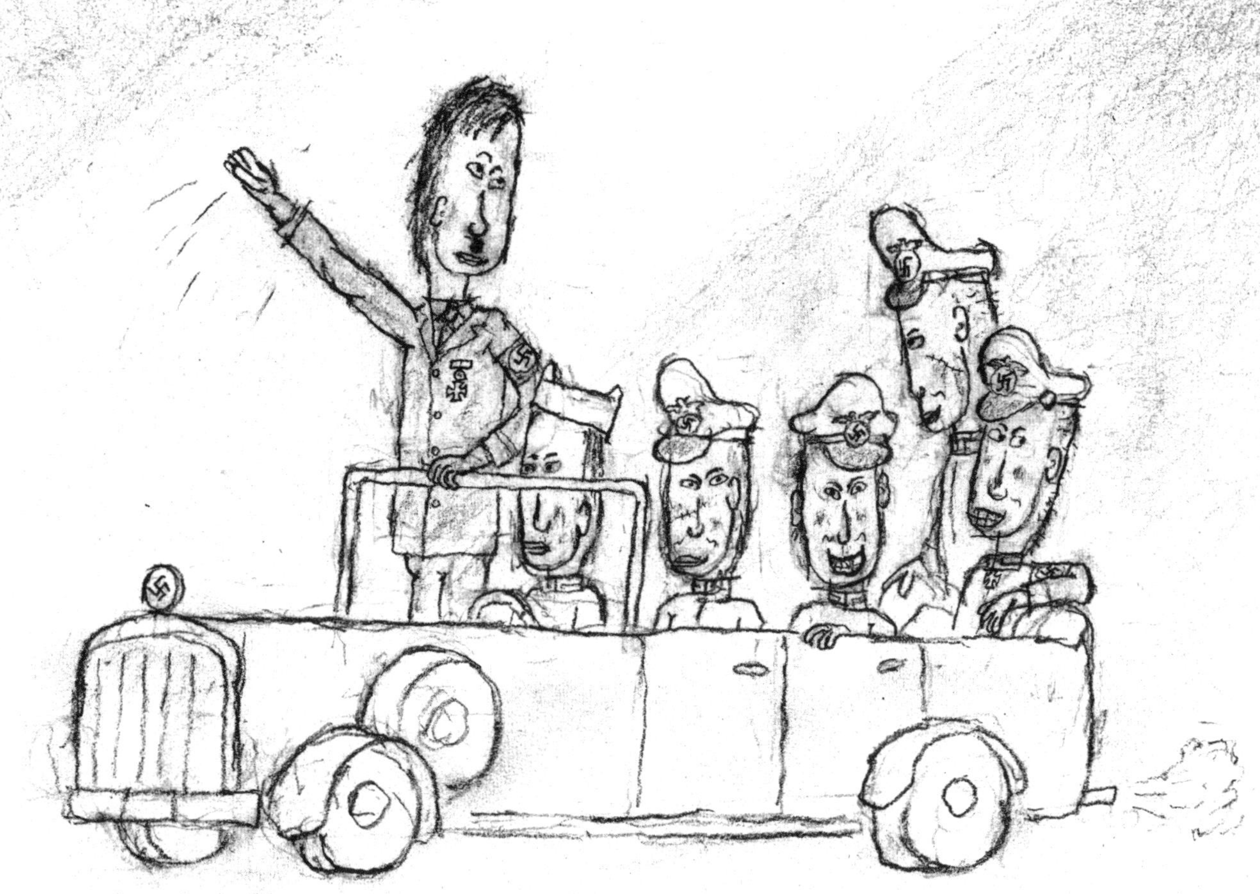

Kraut officers were all
born with big dueling scars
on their faces.

Their favorite word was:

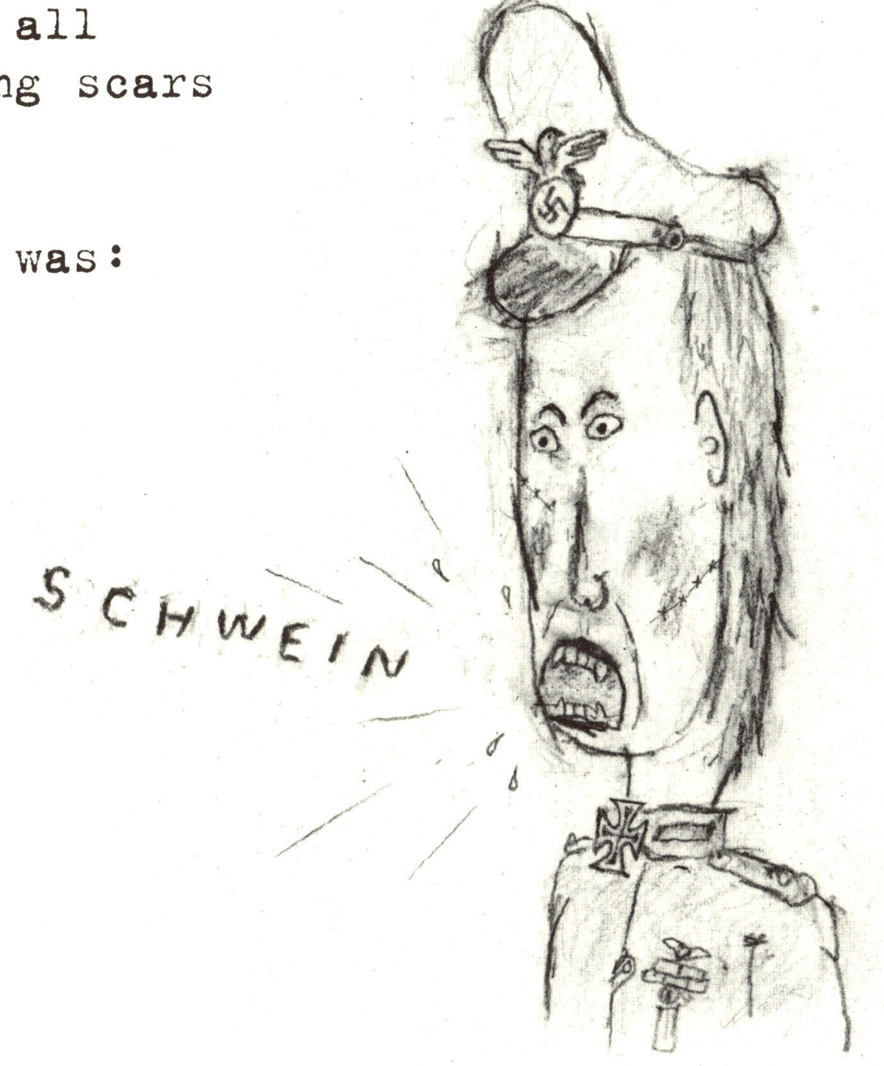

Whenever Hitler conquered a new country, he would do a dance.

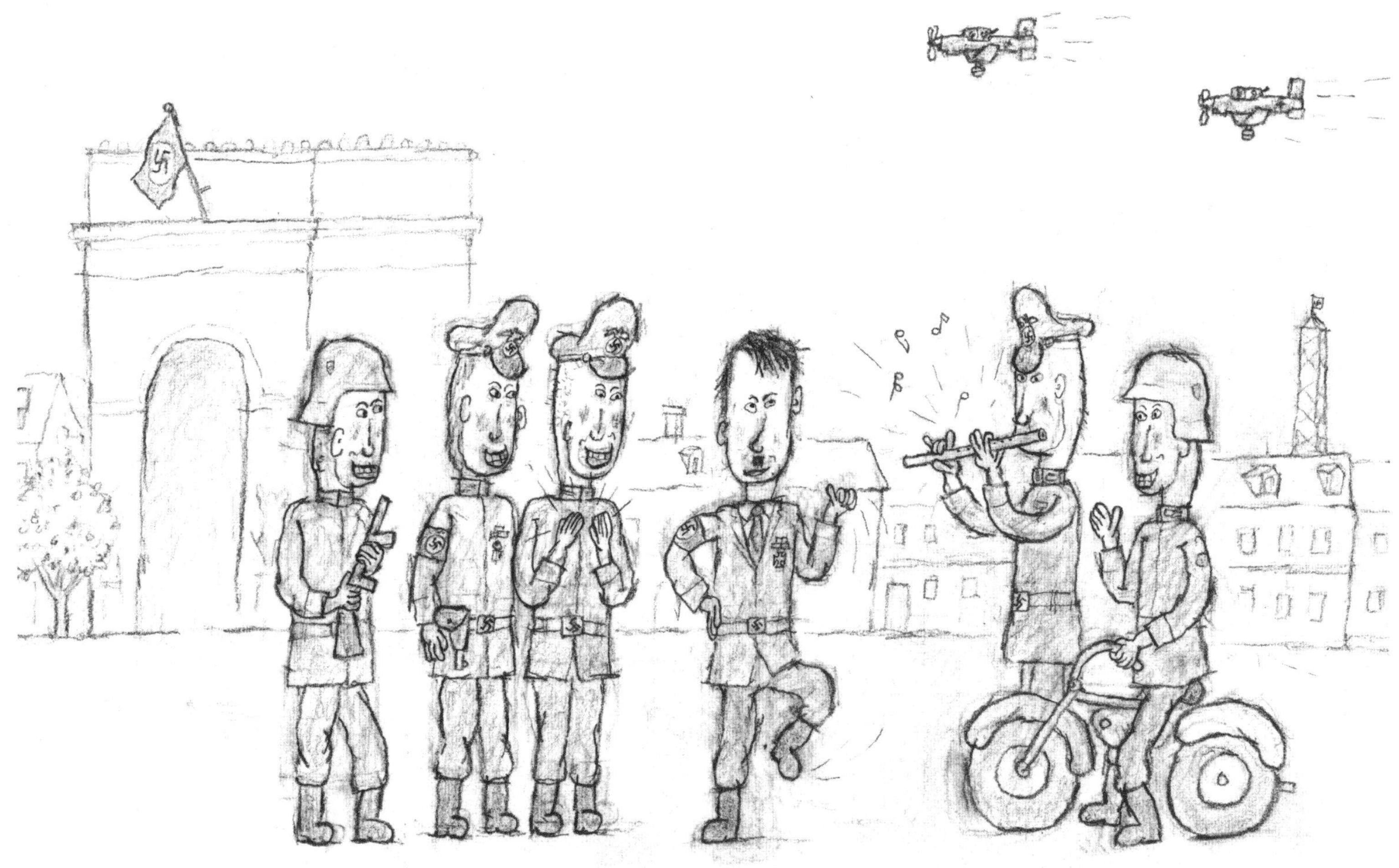

The Luftwaffe featured Hitler's
favorite plane, the Stuka.

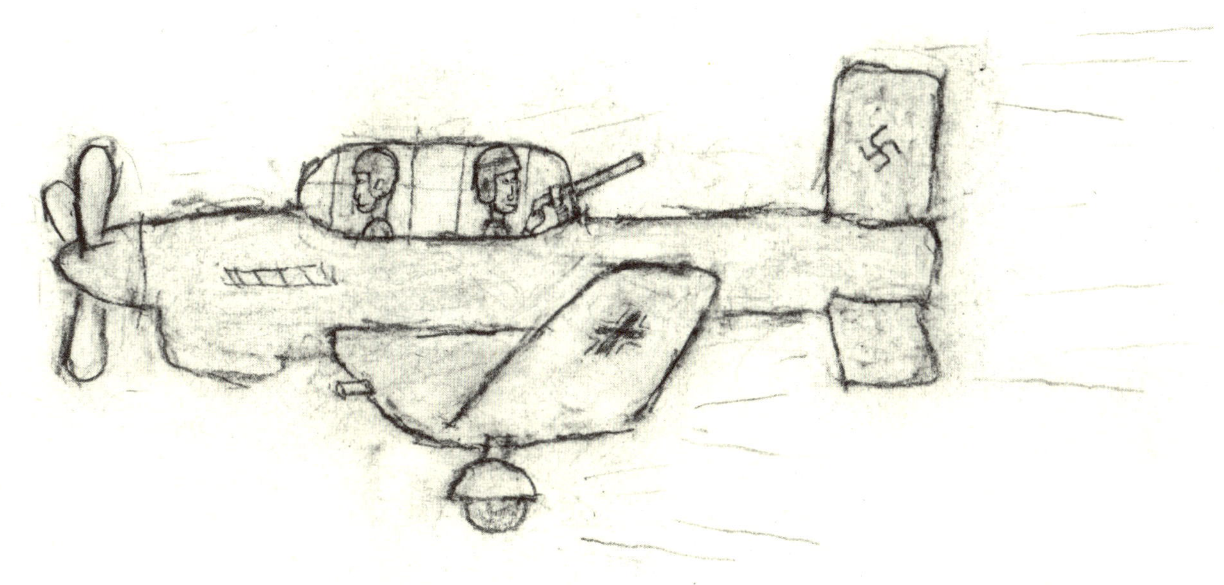

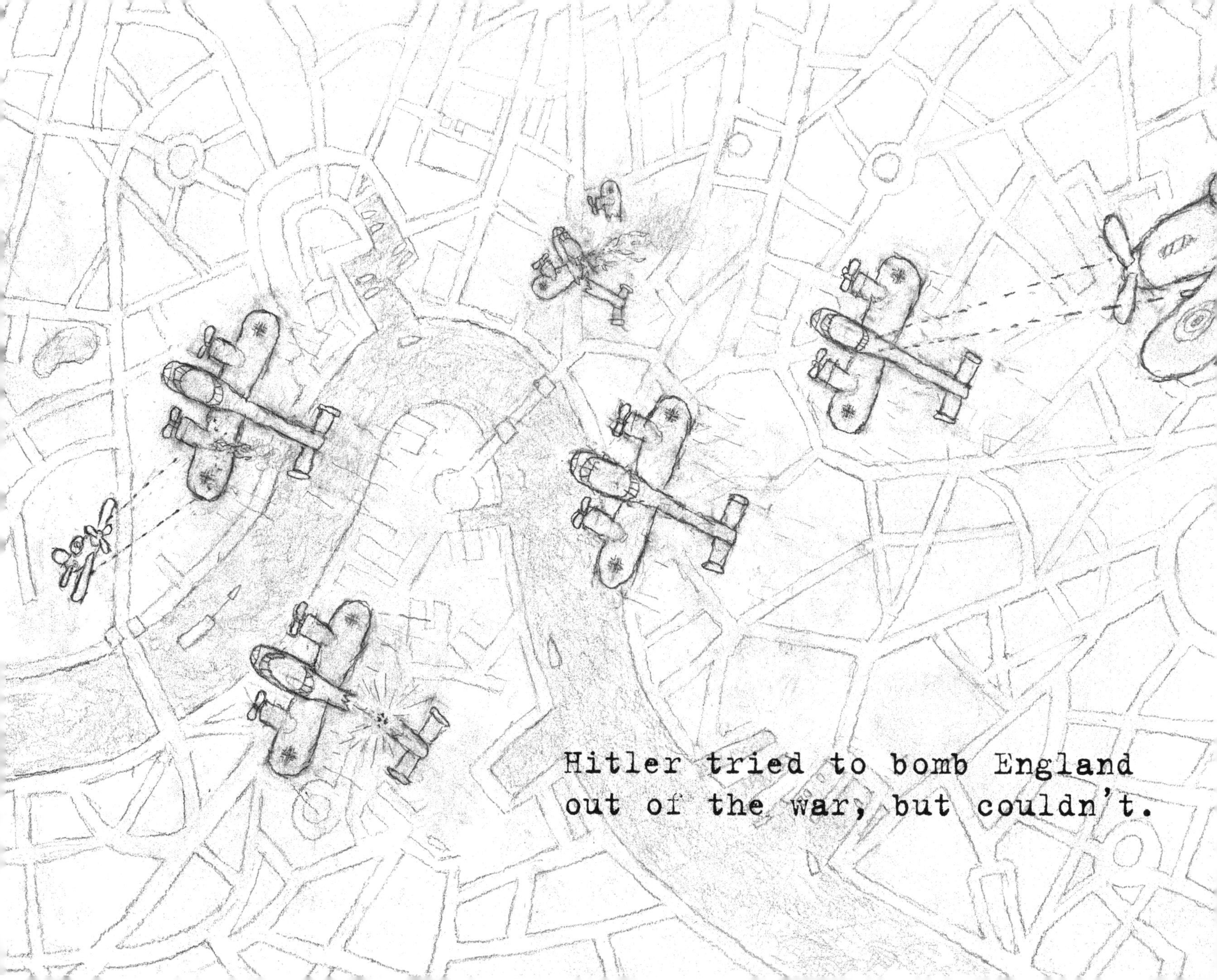

Hitler tried to bomb England
out of the war, but couldn't.

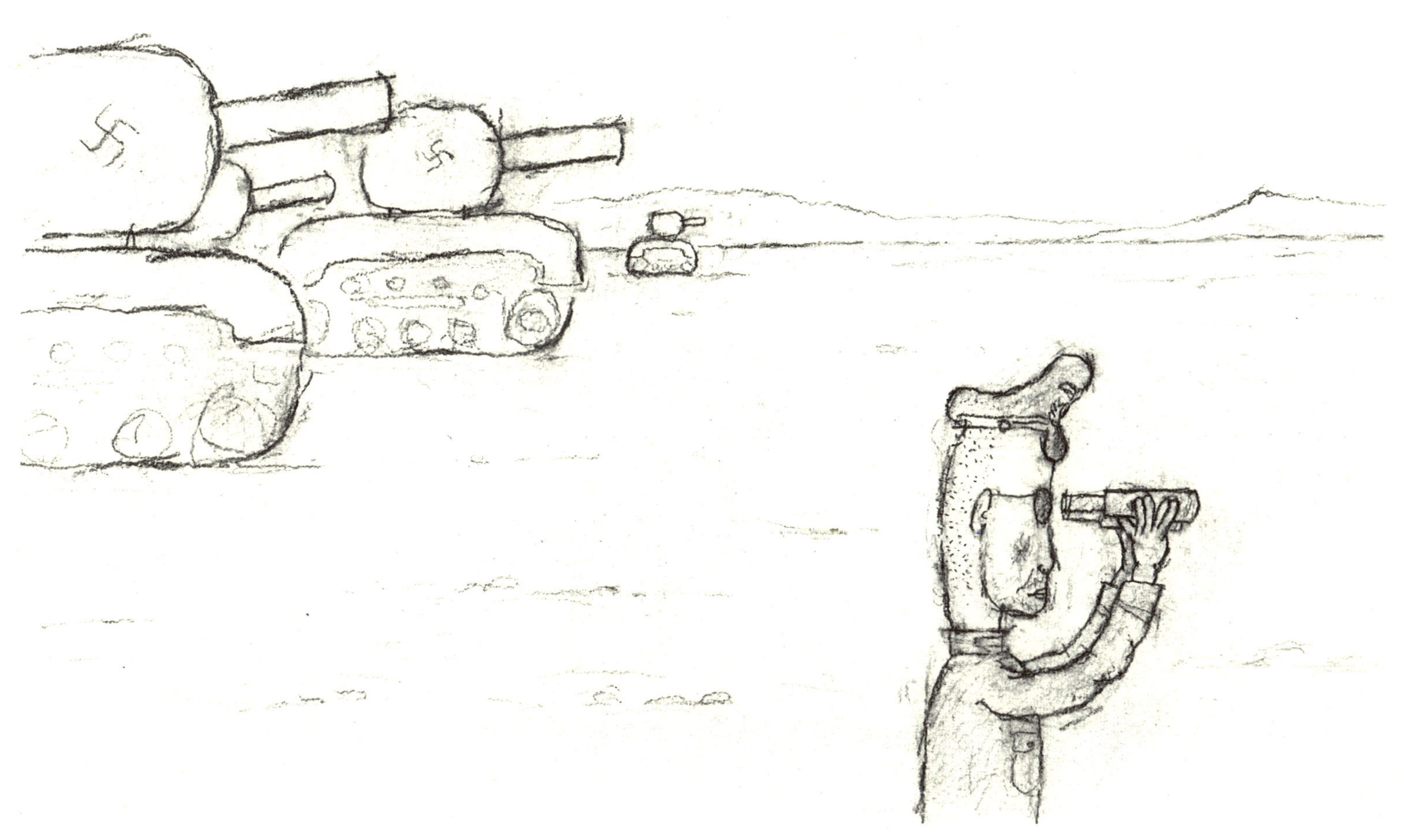

The Allies had to fight
Rommel, the desert fox.

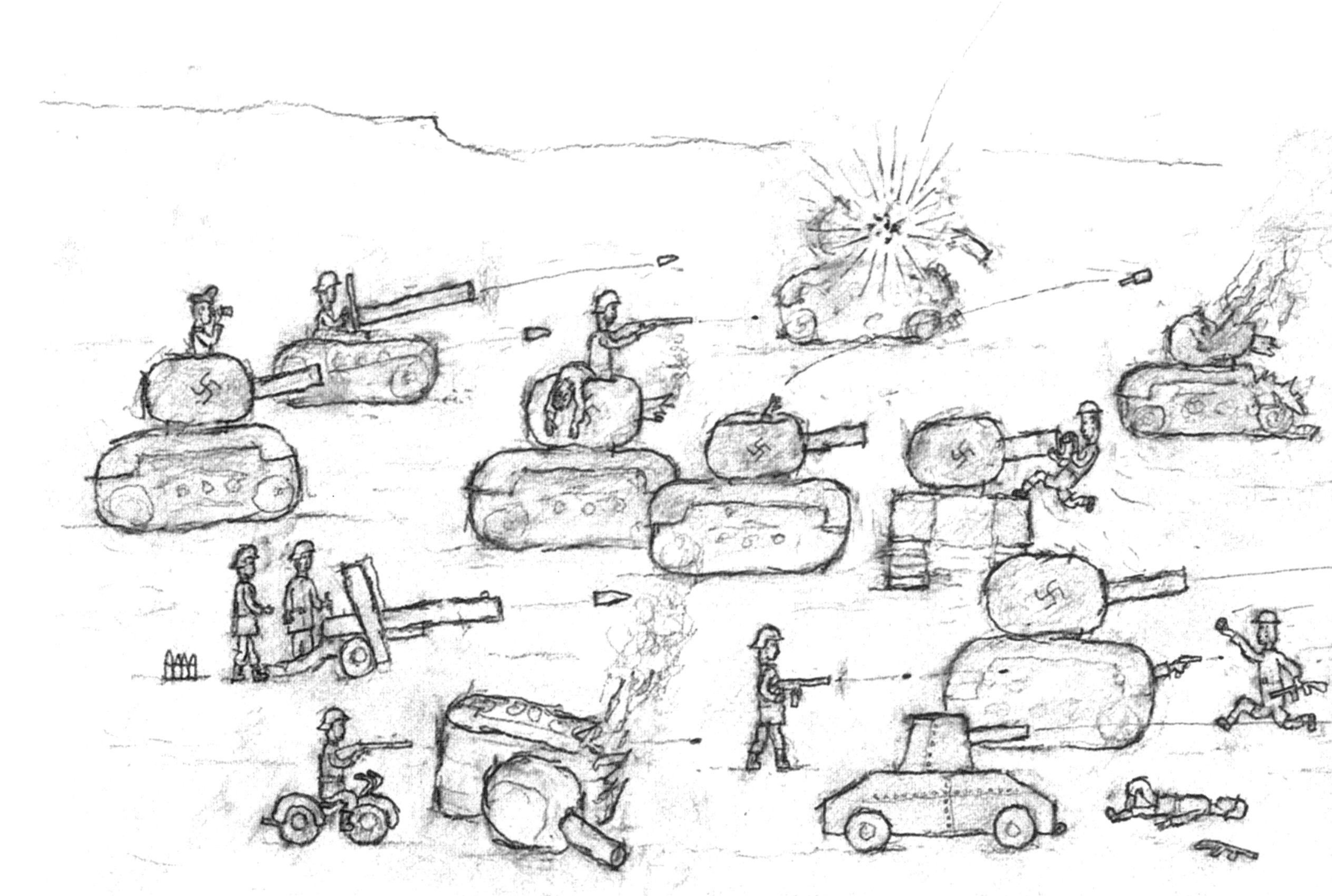

EL ALAMEIN

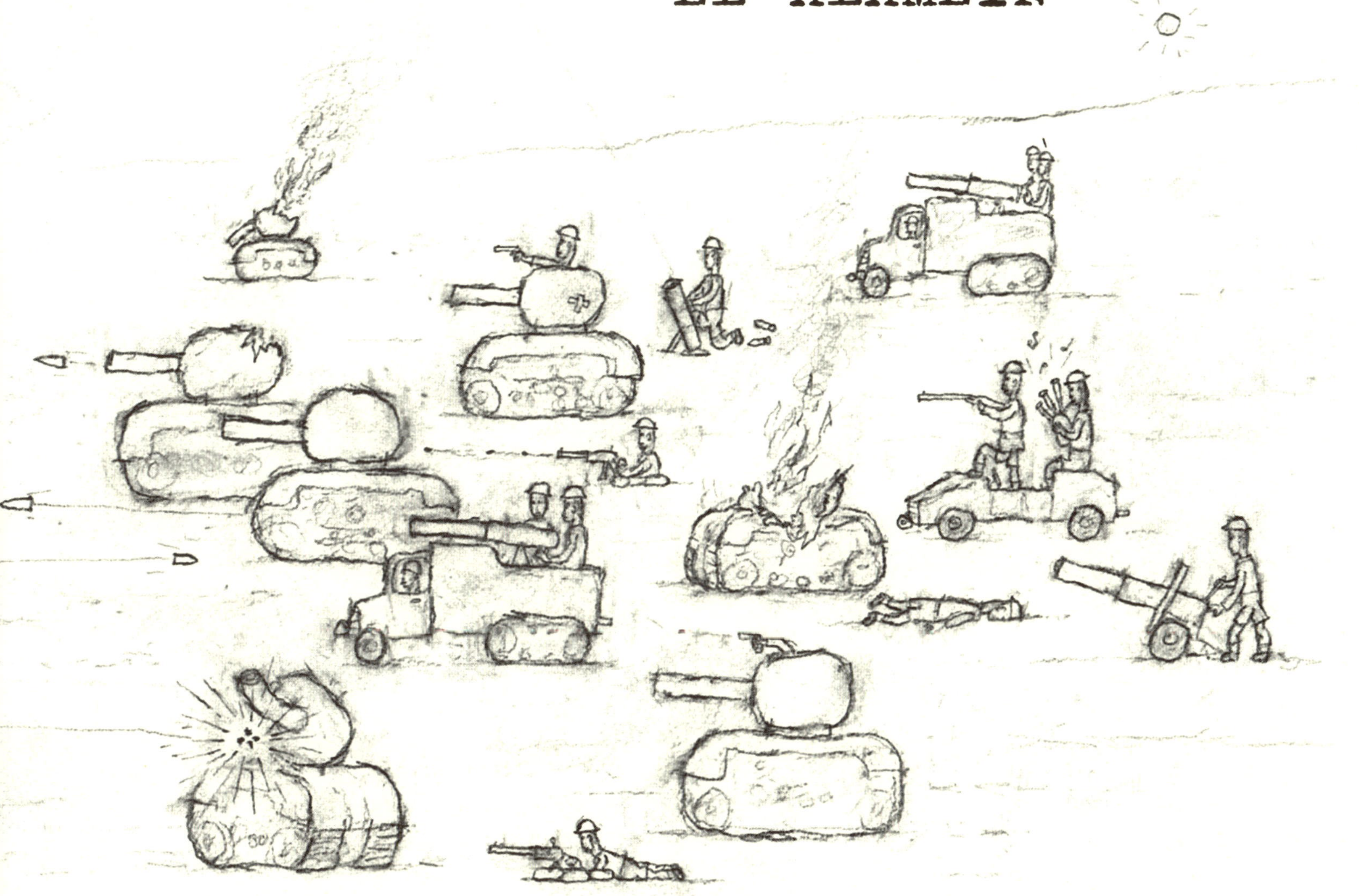

Afterwards, Rommel took
off for Krautland.

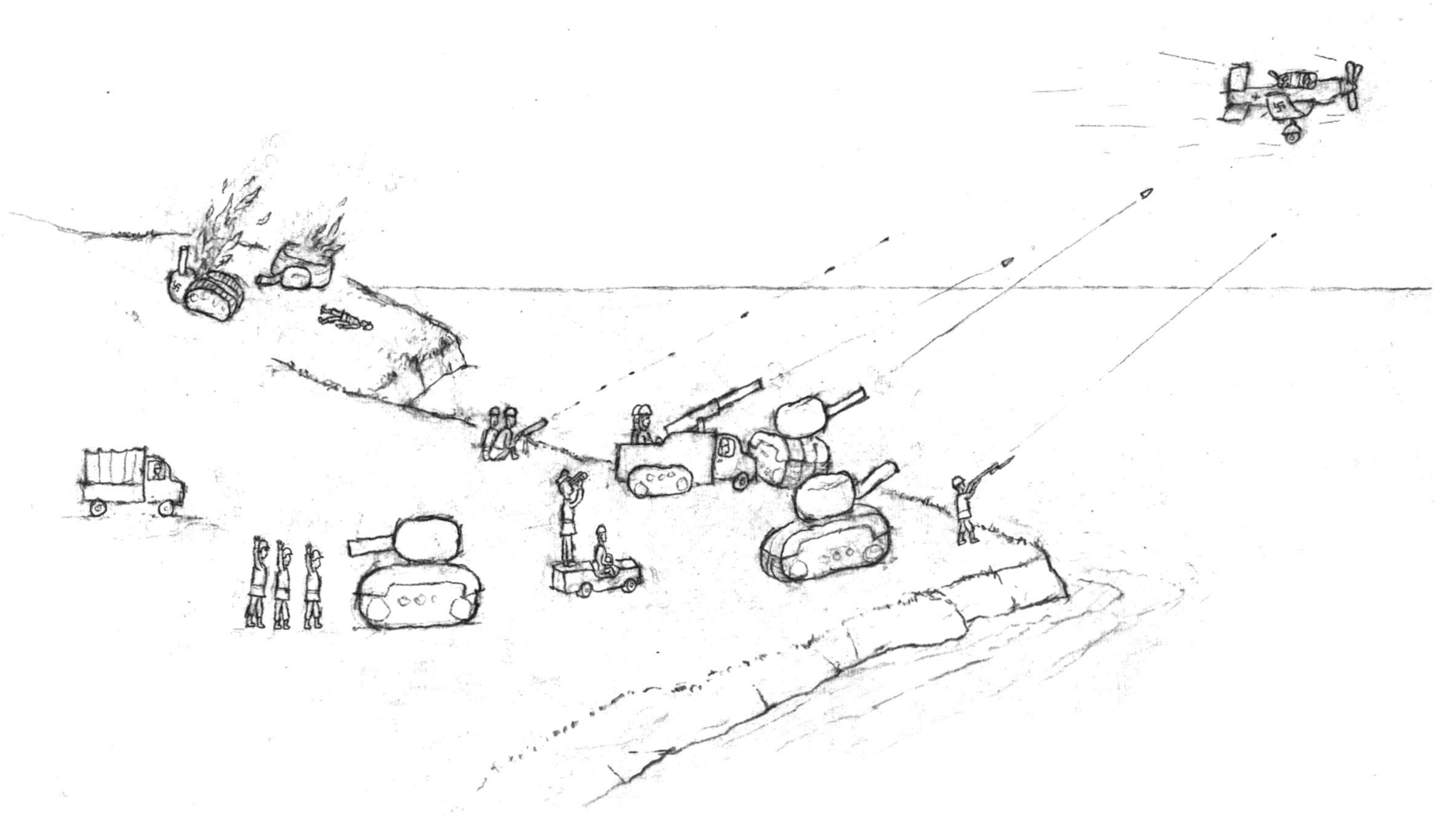

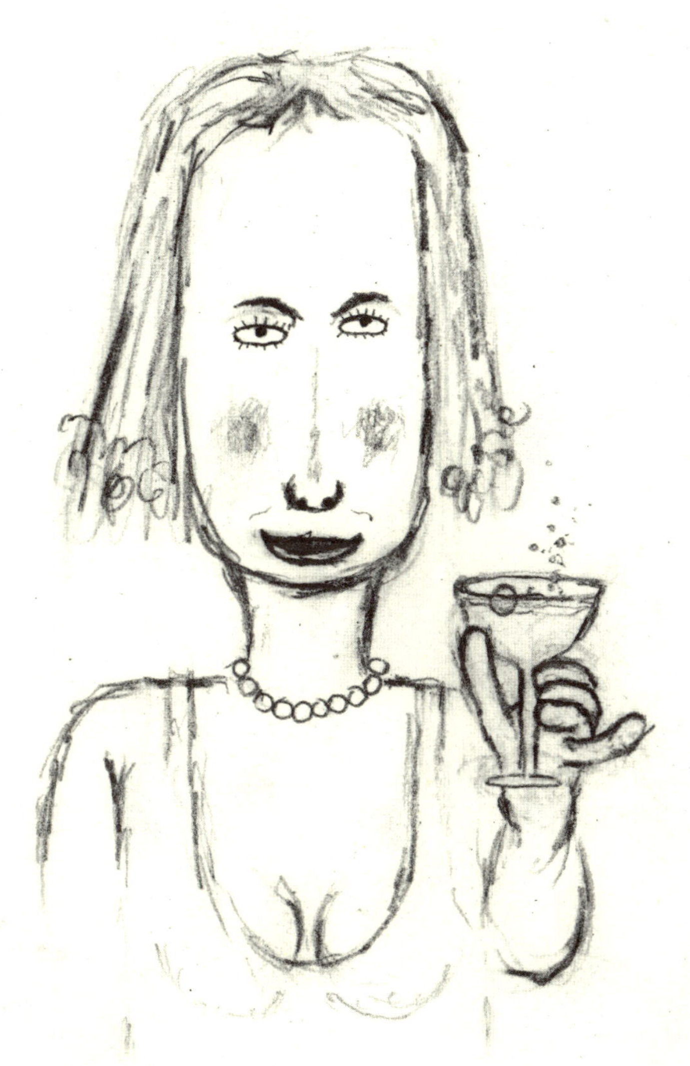

The Nazis had a lot of blond lady spies who liked to get secrets in return for certain favors. Then they would tell U-boat commanders.

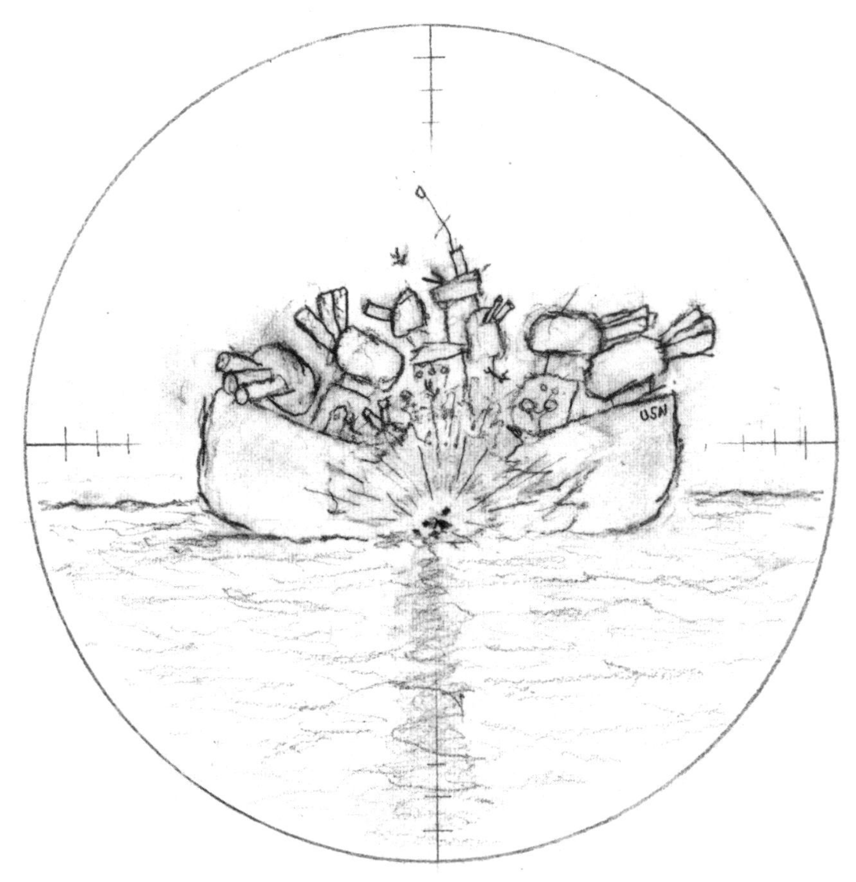

Then here's what would happen.

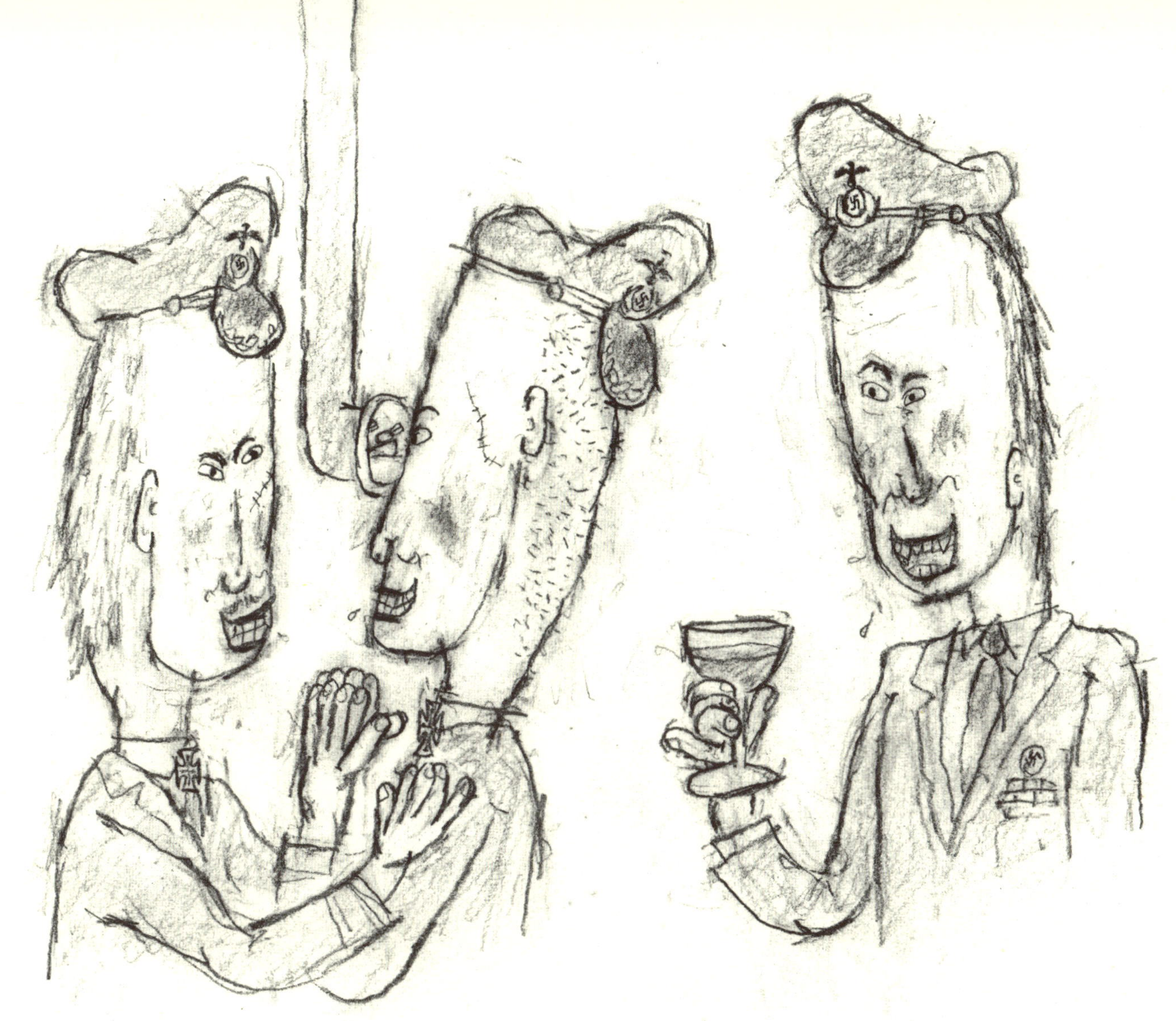

Party time.

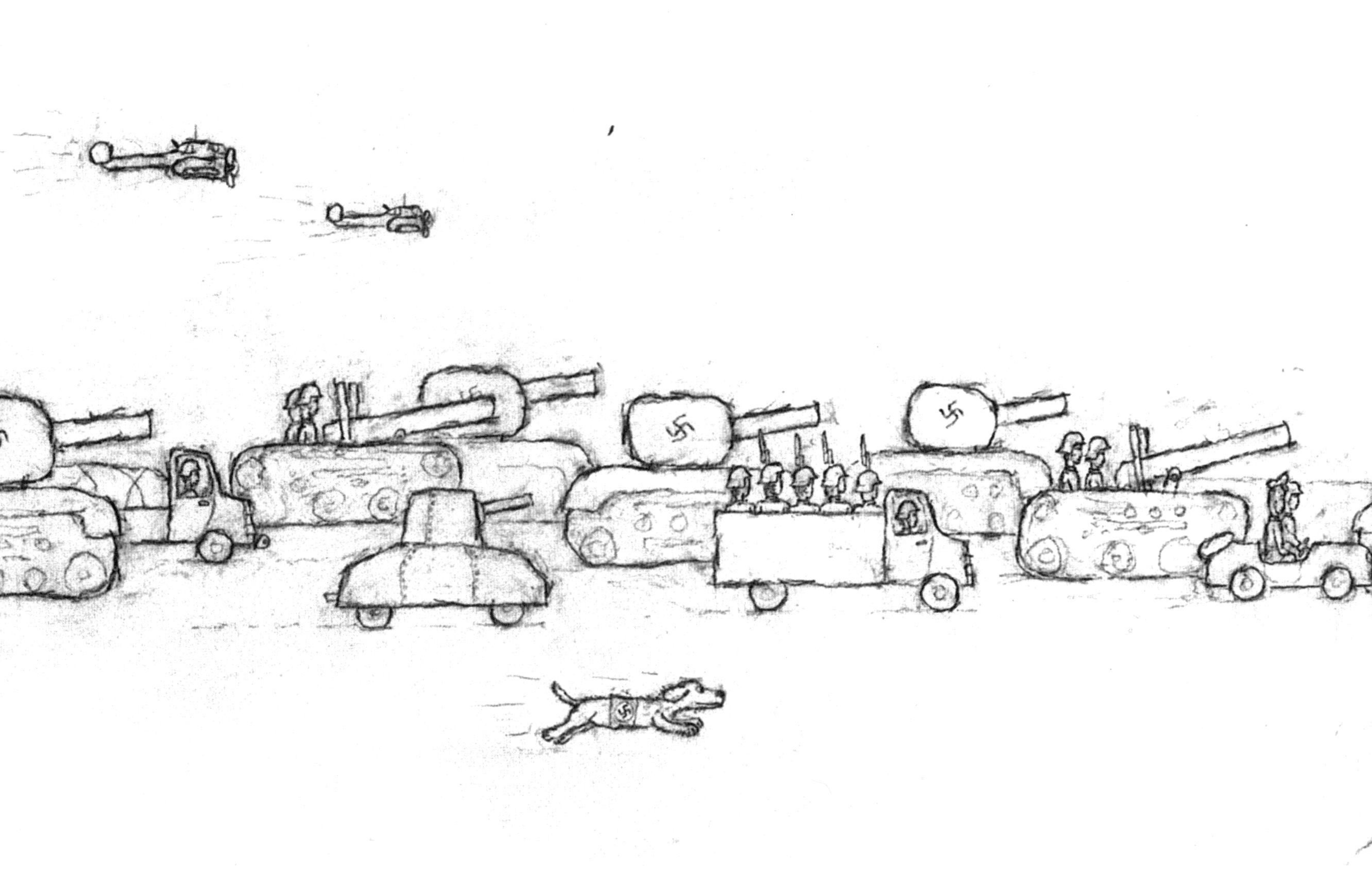

Hitler took it into his head to
sic the Wehrmacht on Russia, except
then they got to Stalingrad.

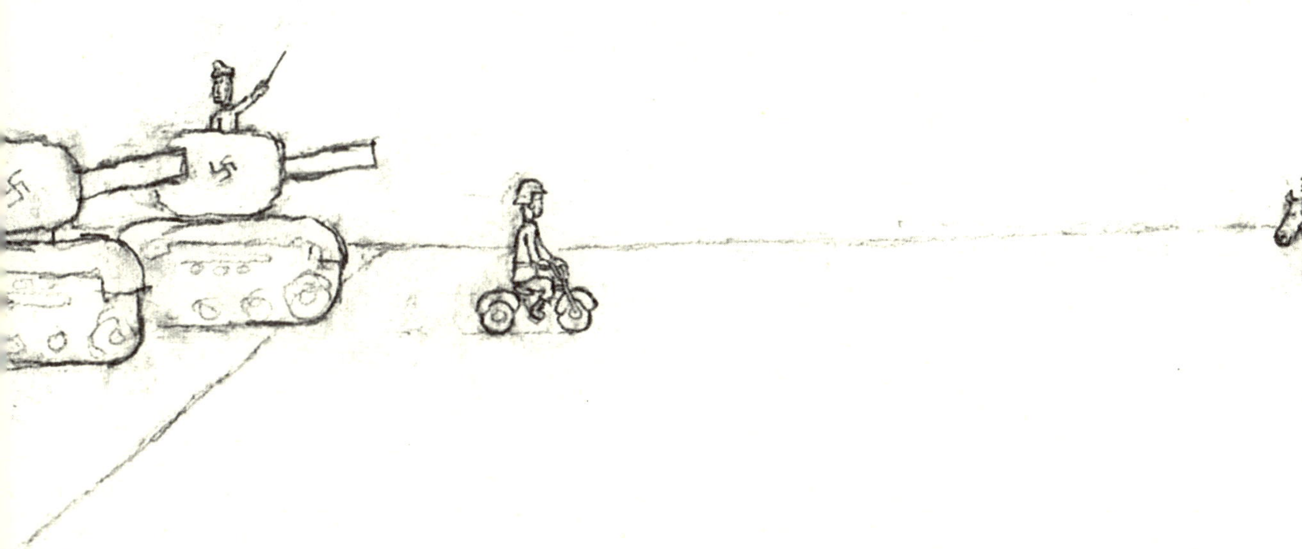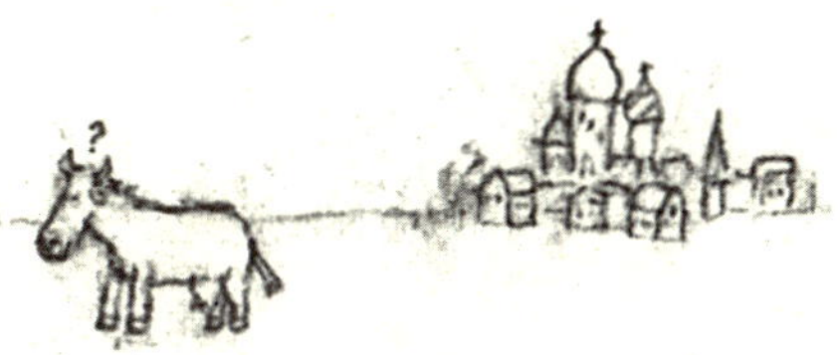

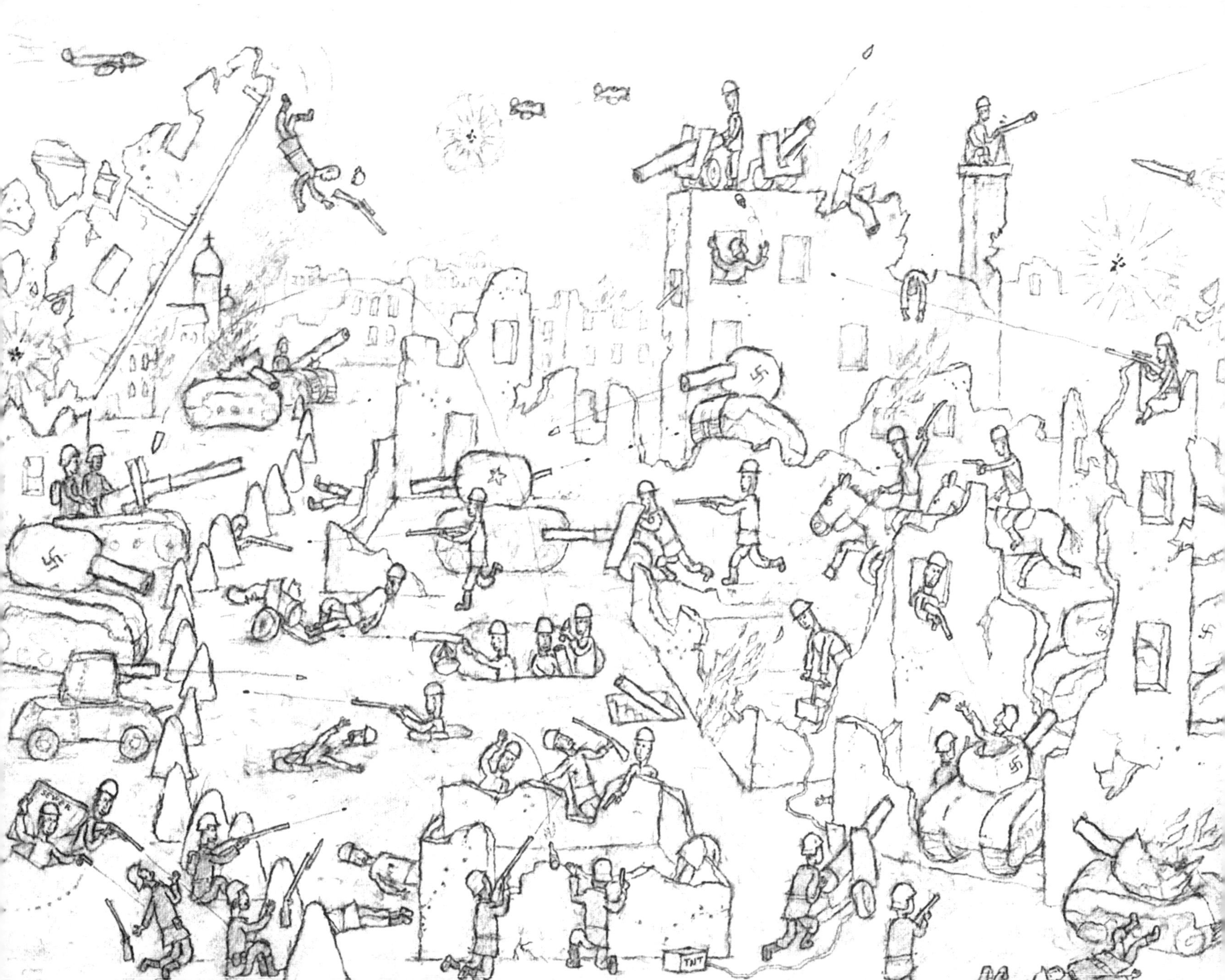
SEWER
TNT

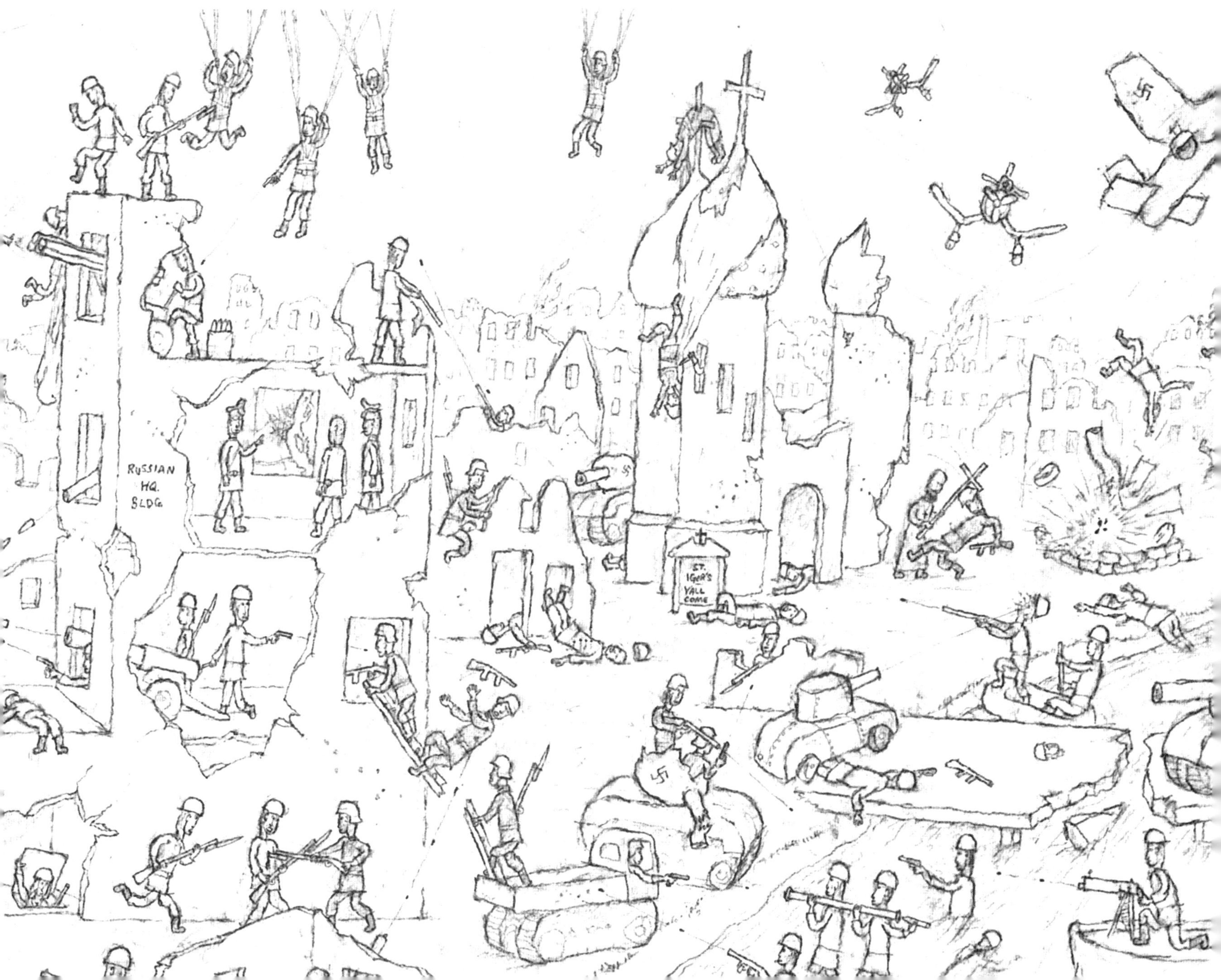

RUSSIAN HQ. BLDG
ST. IGOR'S — YALL COME

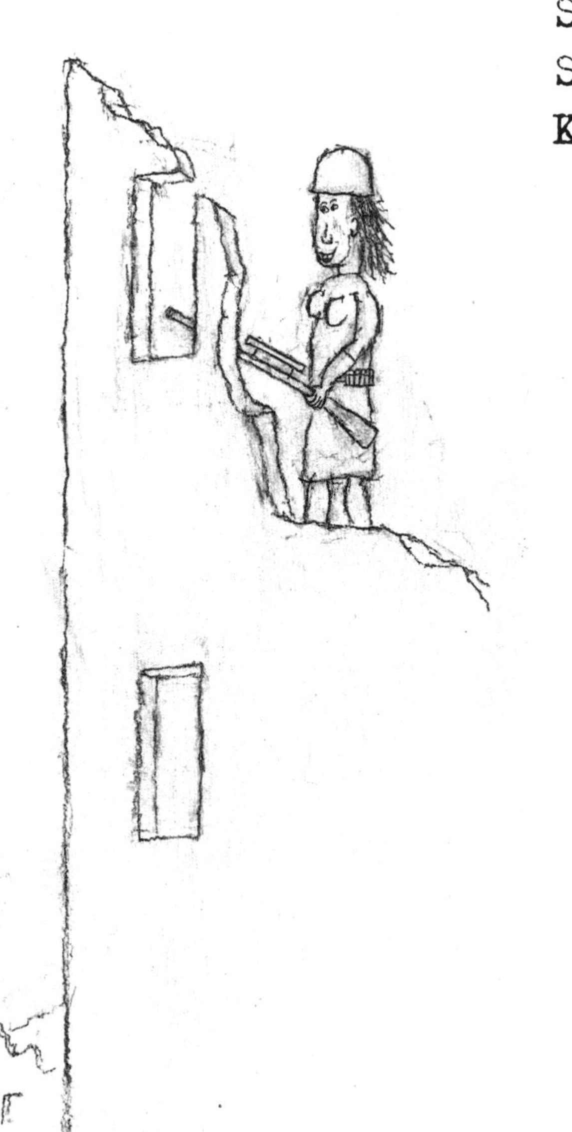

Sniper Tania Chernova.
She wiped out 80
Krauts.

The German general staff
got the news from
Stalingrad

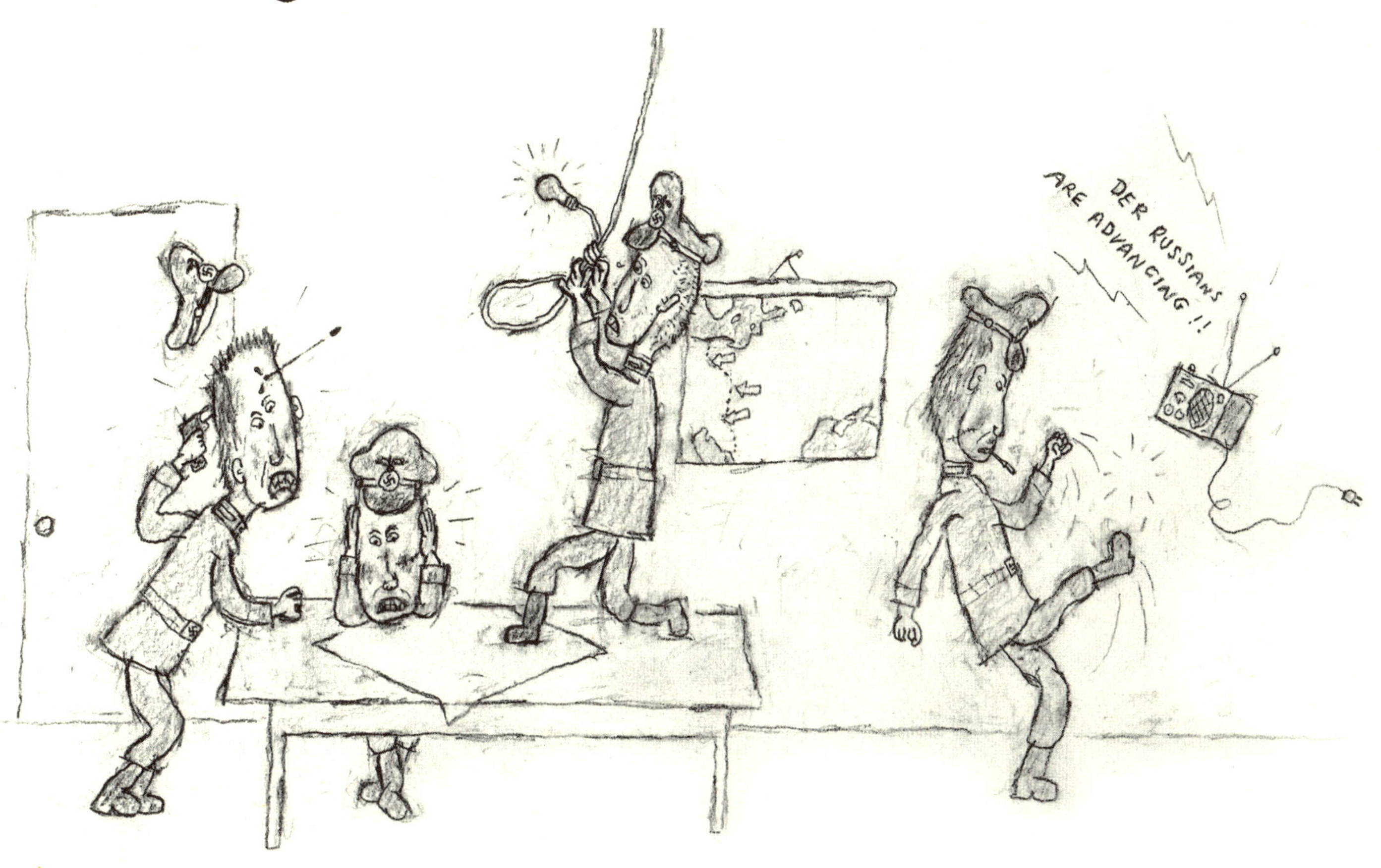

Meanwhile the partisans
were giving it to the huns

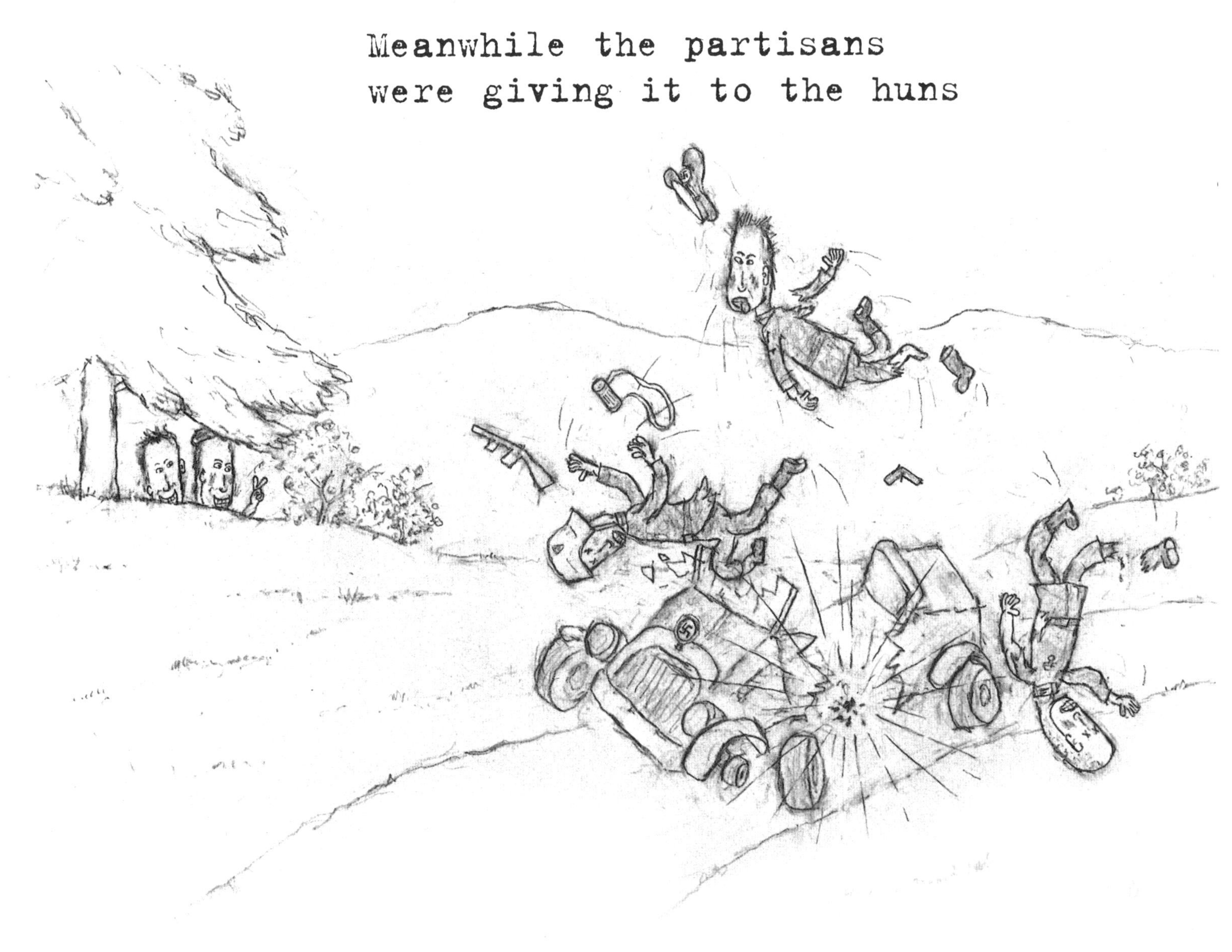

Sometimes the Katzenjammer boys caught a Partisan.

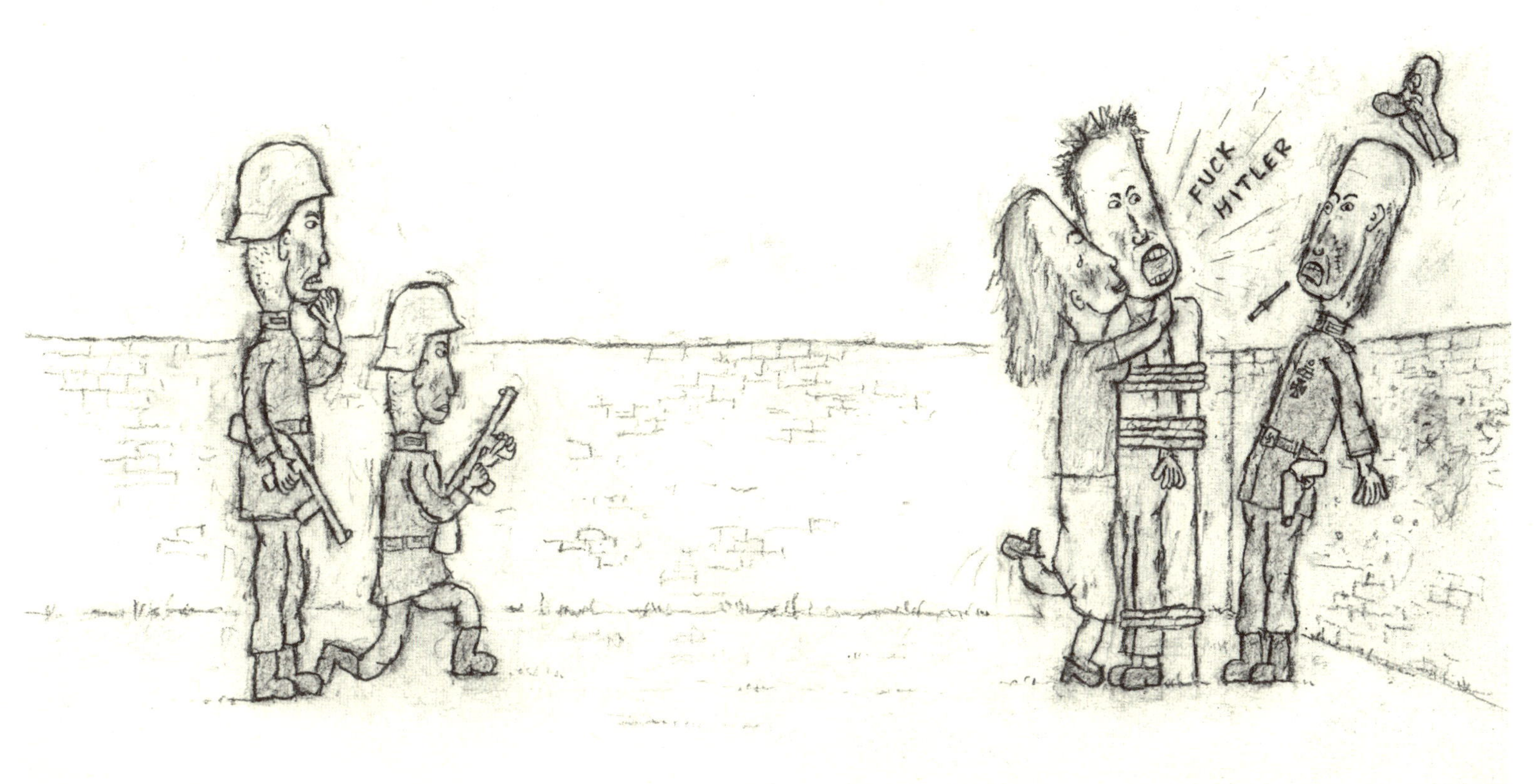

Some
friends
and
some
foes.

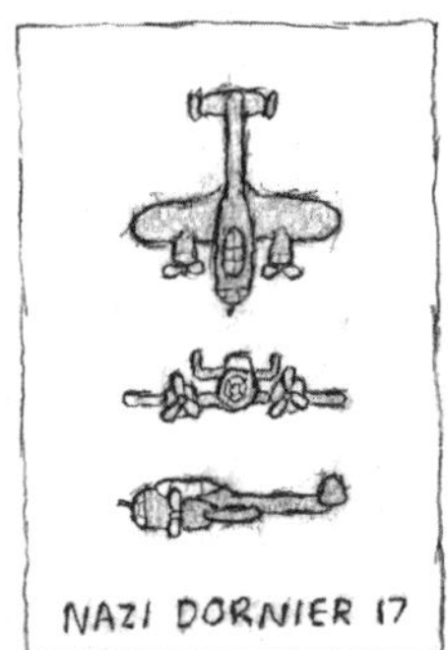

NAZI DORNIER 17

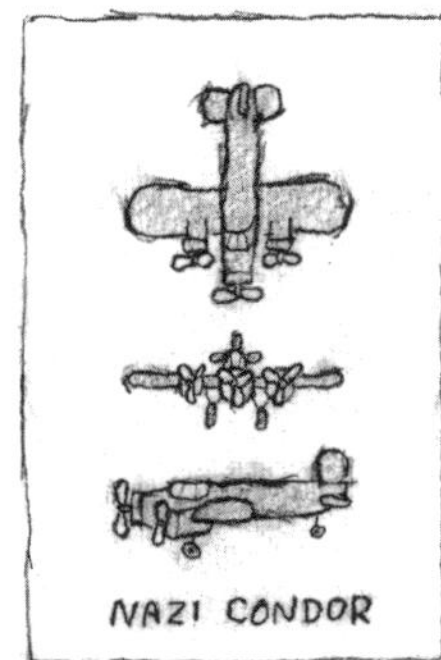

NAZI CONDOR

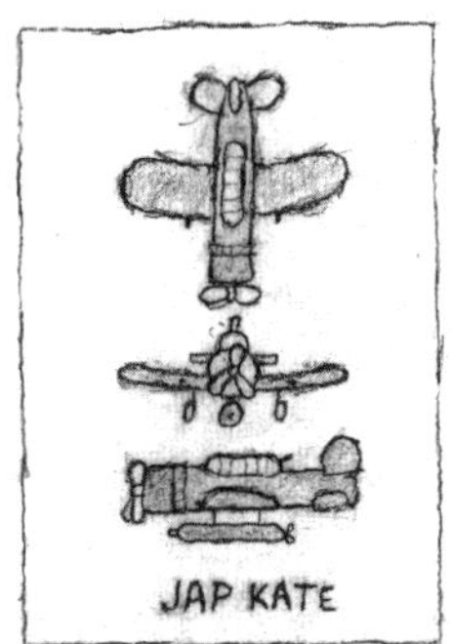

JAP KATE

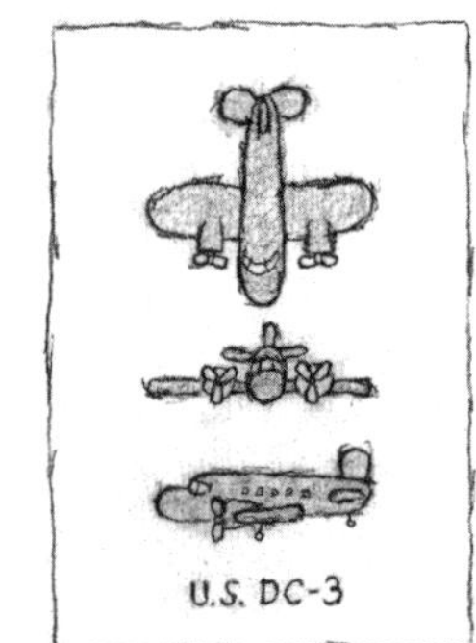

U.S. DC-3

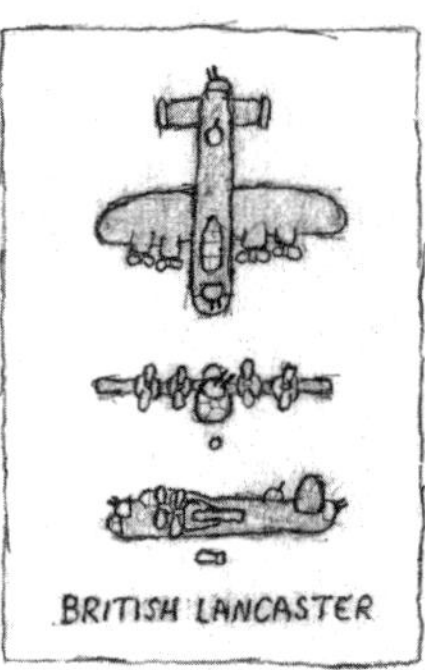

BRITISH LANCASTER

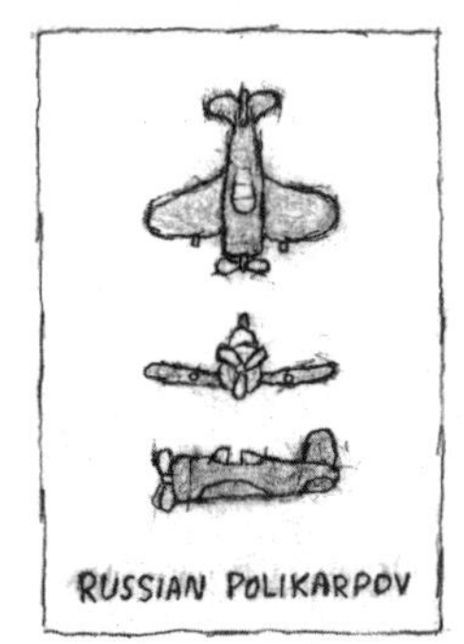

RUSSIAN POLIKARPOV

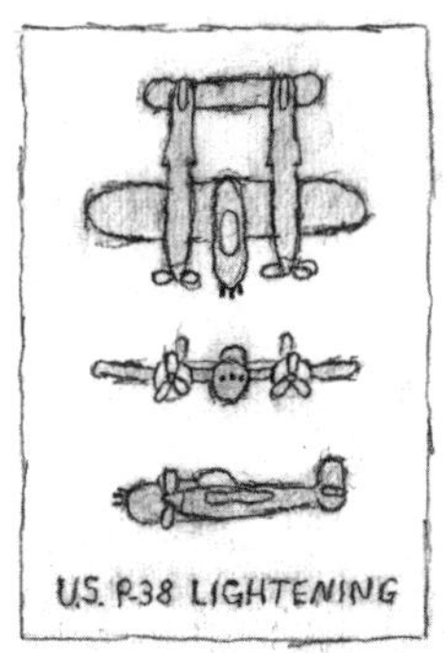

U.S. P-38 LIGHTENING

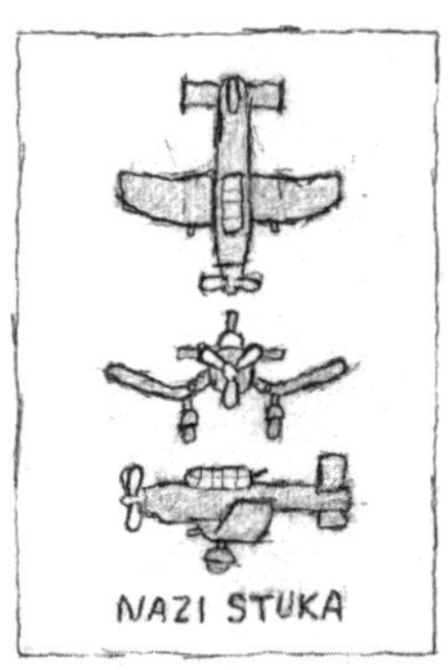

NAZI STUKA

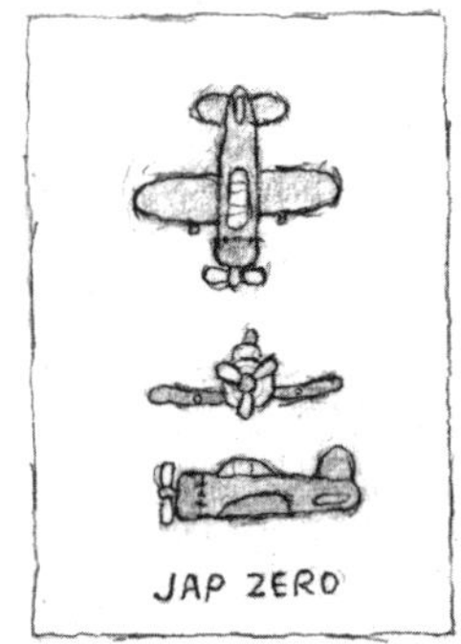

JAP ZERO

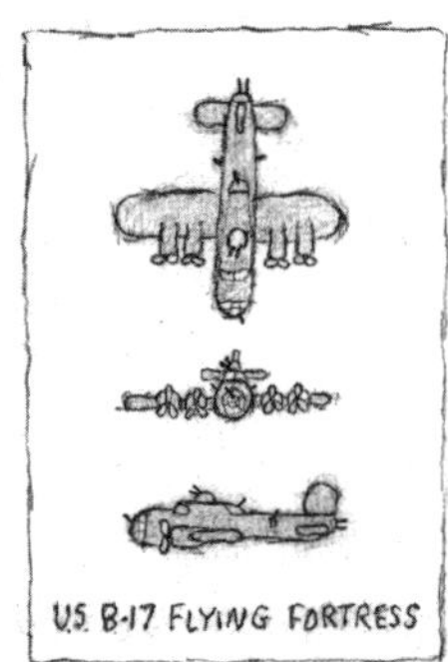

U.S. B-17 FLYING FORTRESS

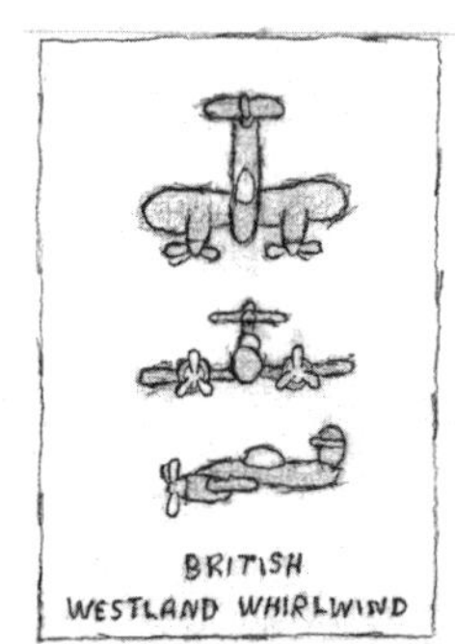

BRITISH
WESTLAND WHIRLWIND

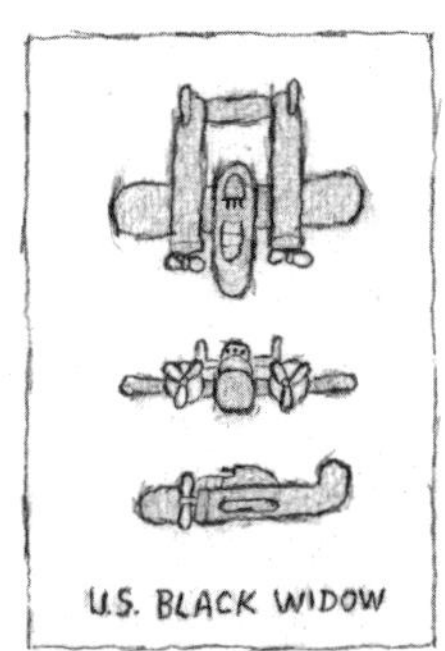

U.S. BLACK WIDOW

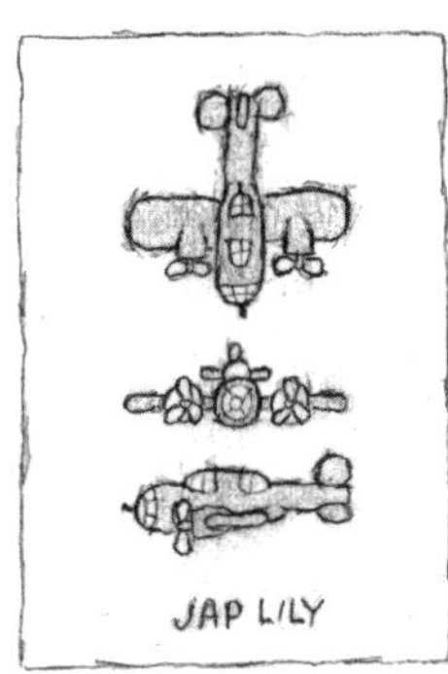

JAP LILY

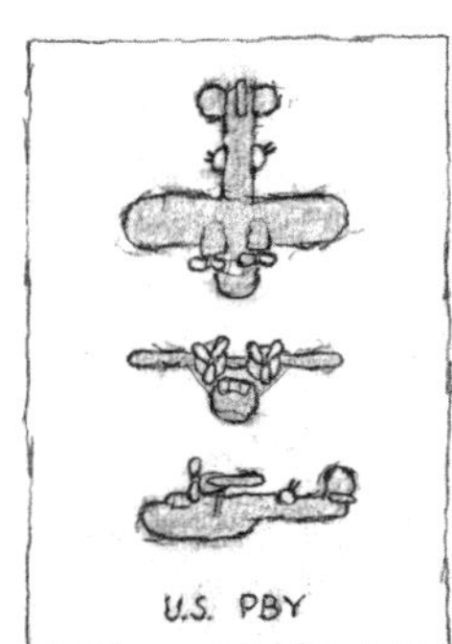

U.S. PBY

Meanwhile, back at the
Jap Theater of War . . .

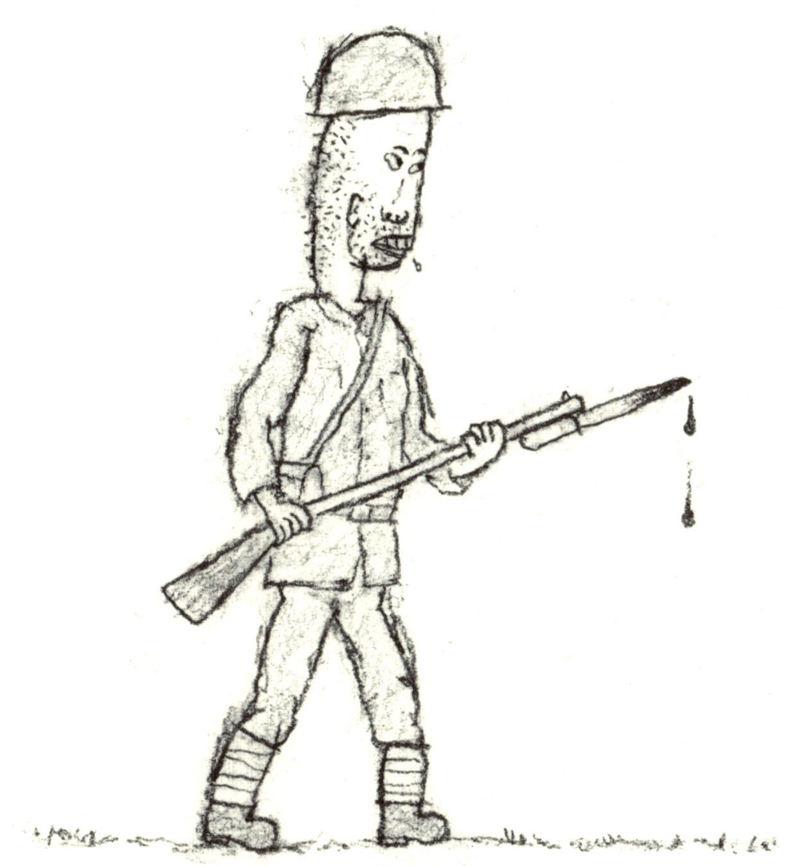

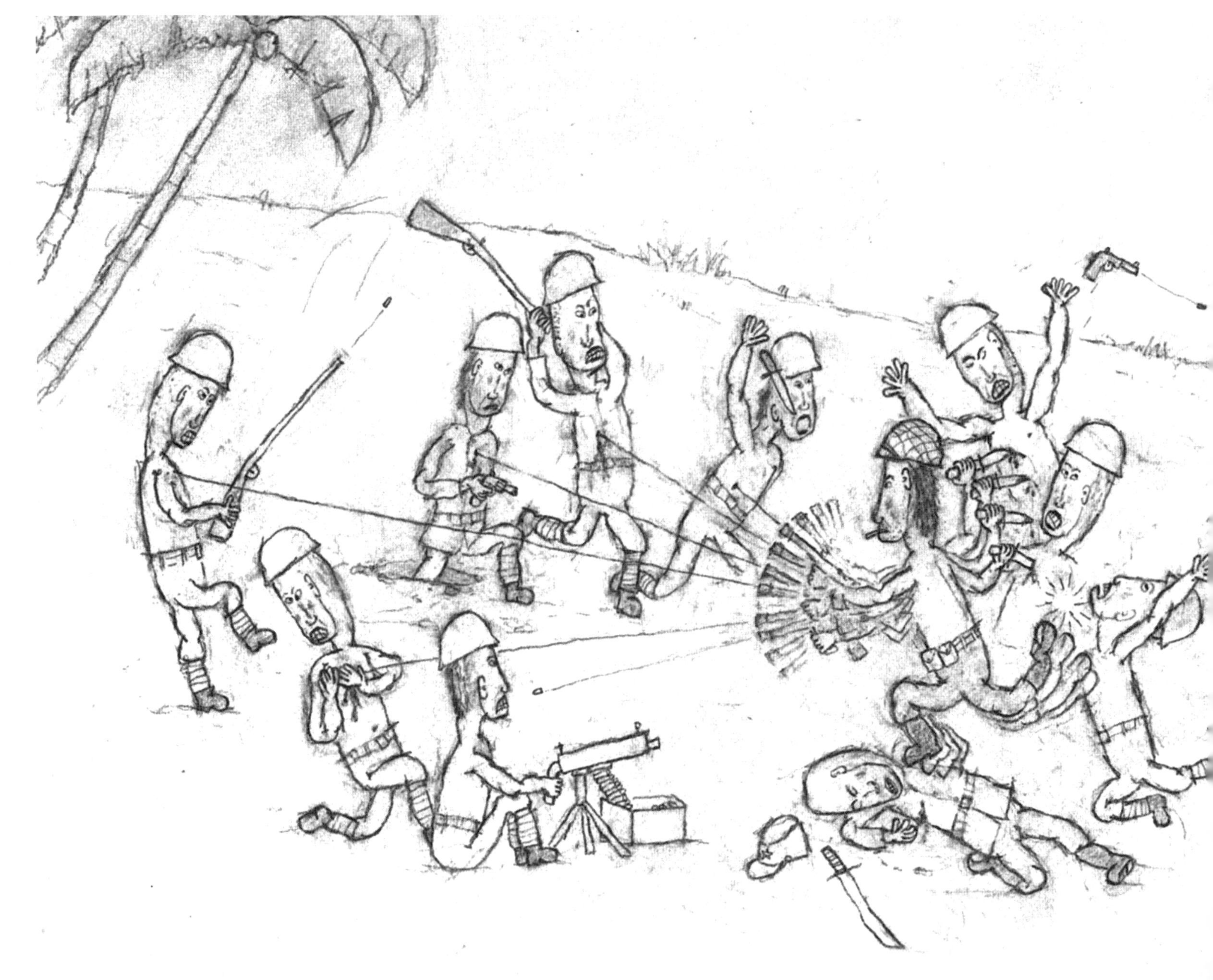

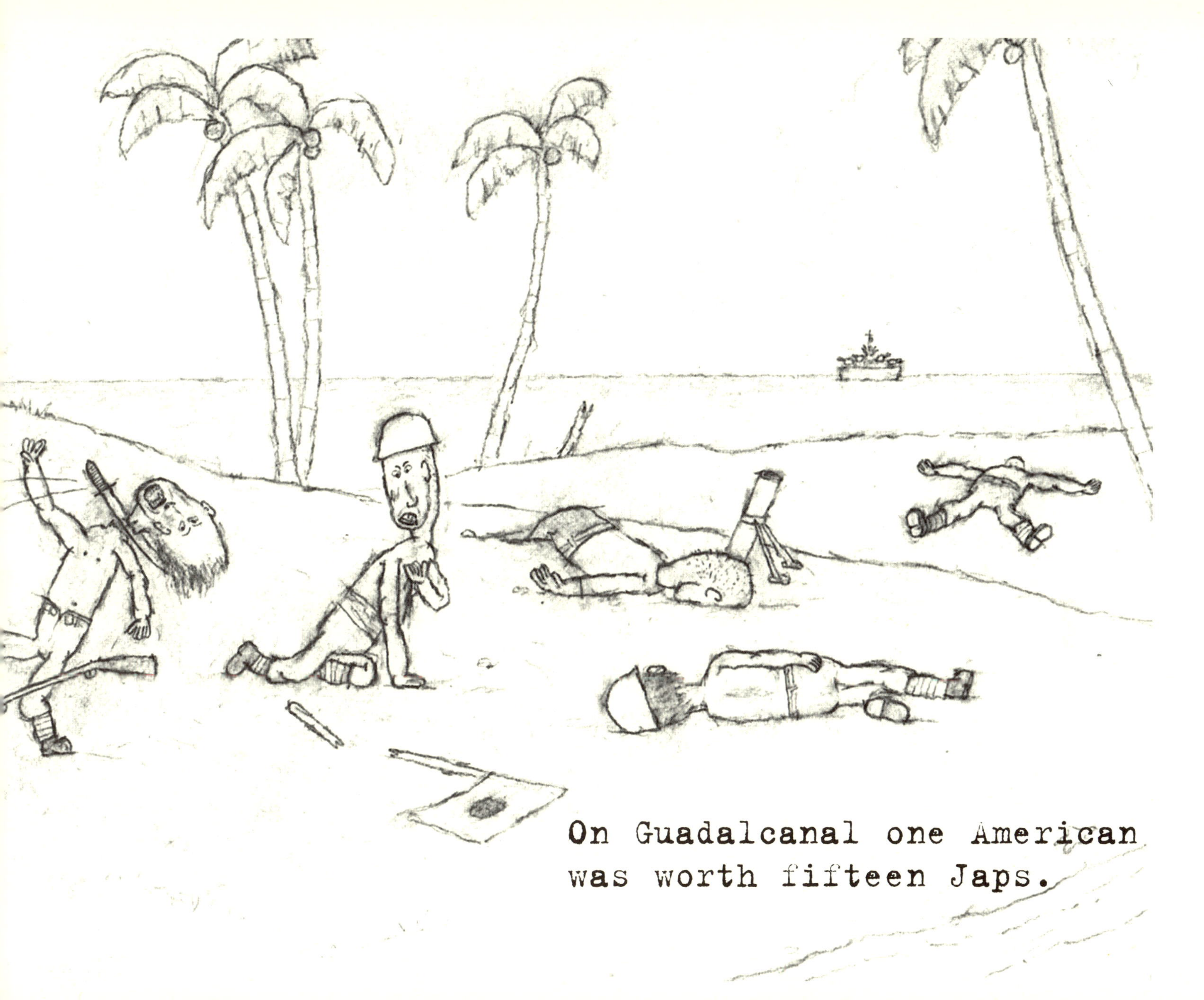

On Guadalcanal one American
was worth fifteen Japs.

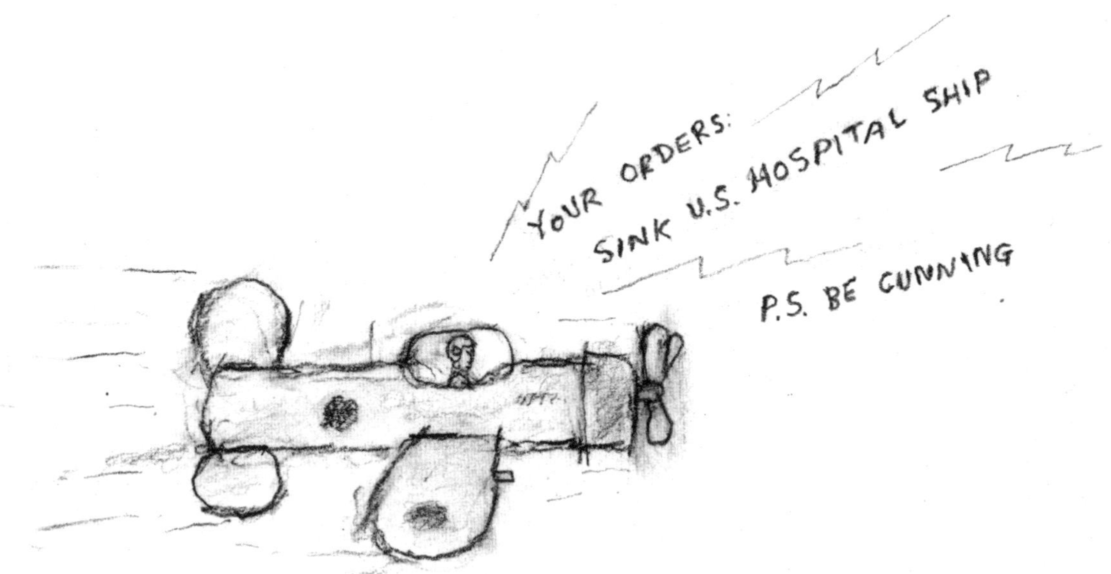

The Jap Zero versus . . .

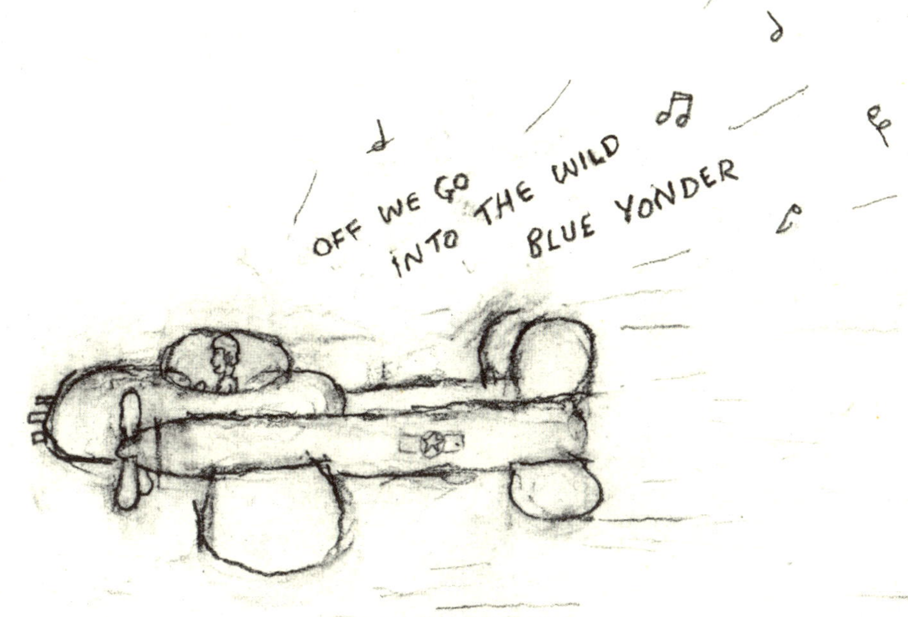

. . . The American P-38.

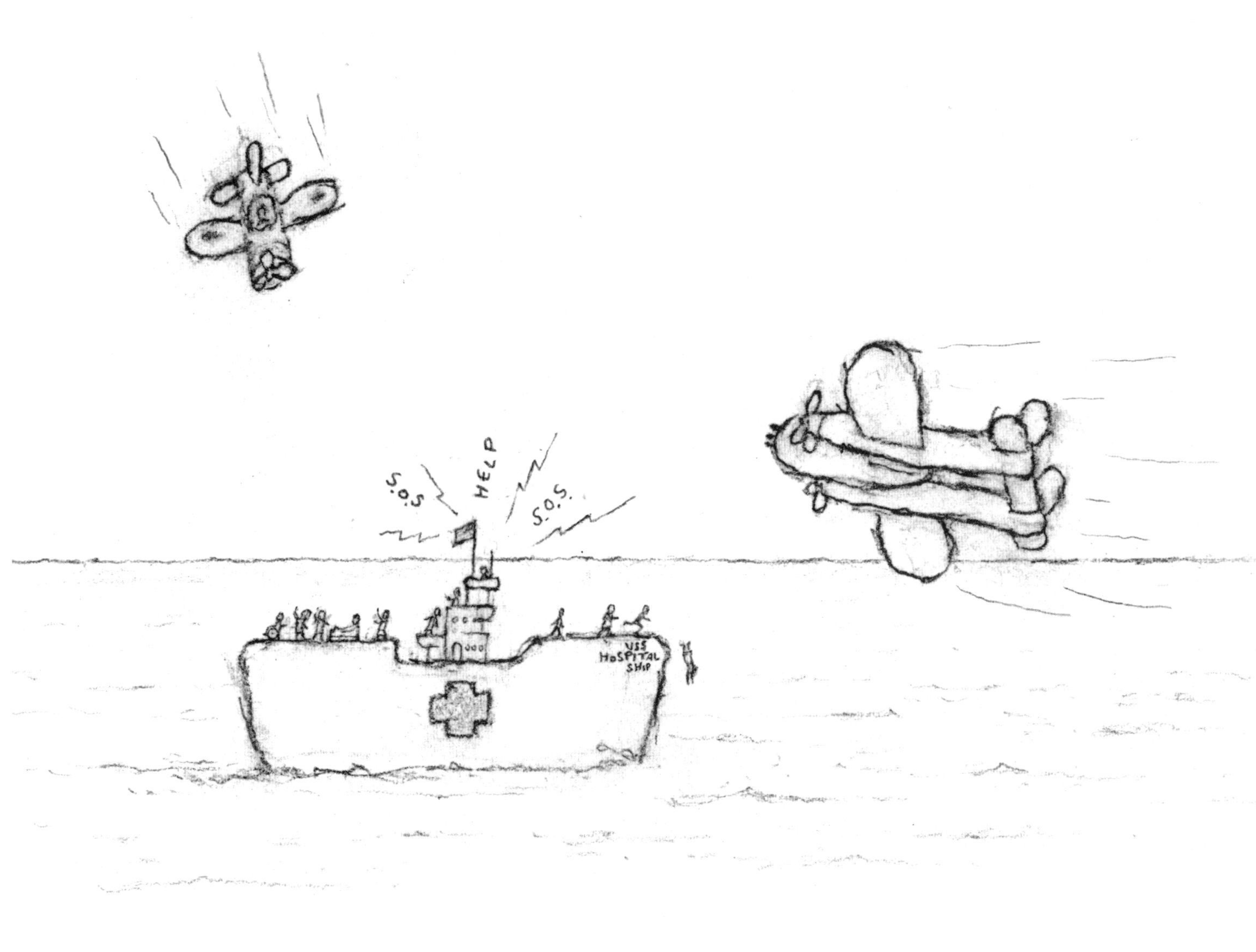

S.O.S
HELP
S.O.S.
USS
HOSPITAL
SHIP

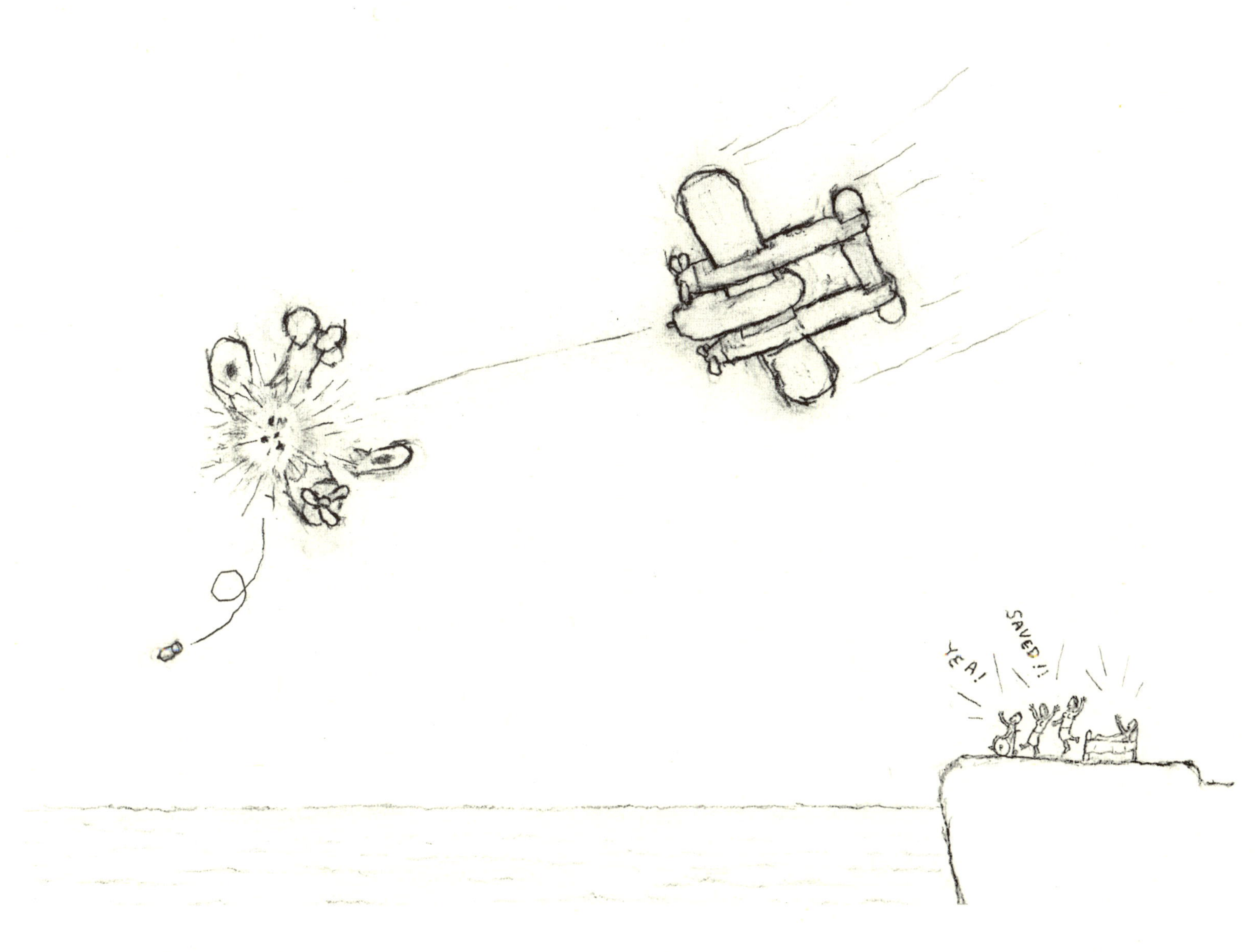

SAVED!!
YEA!

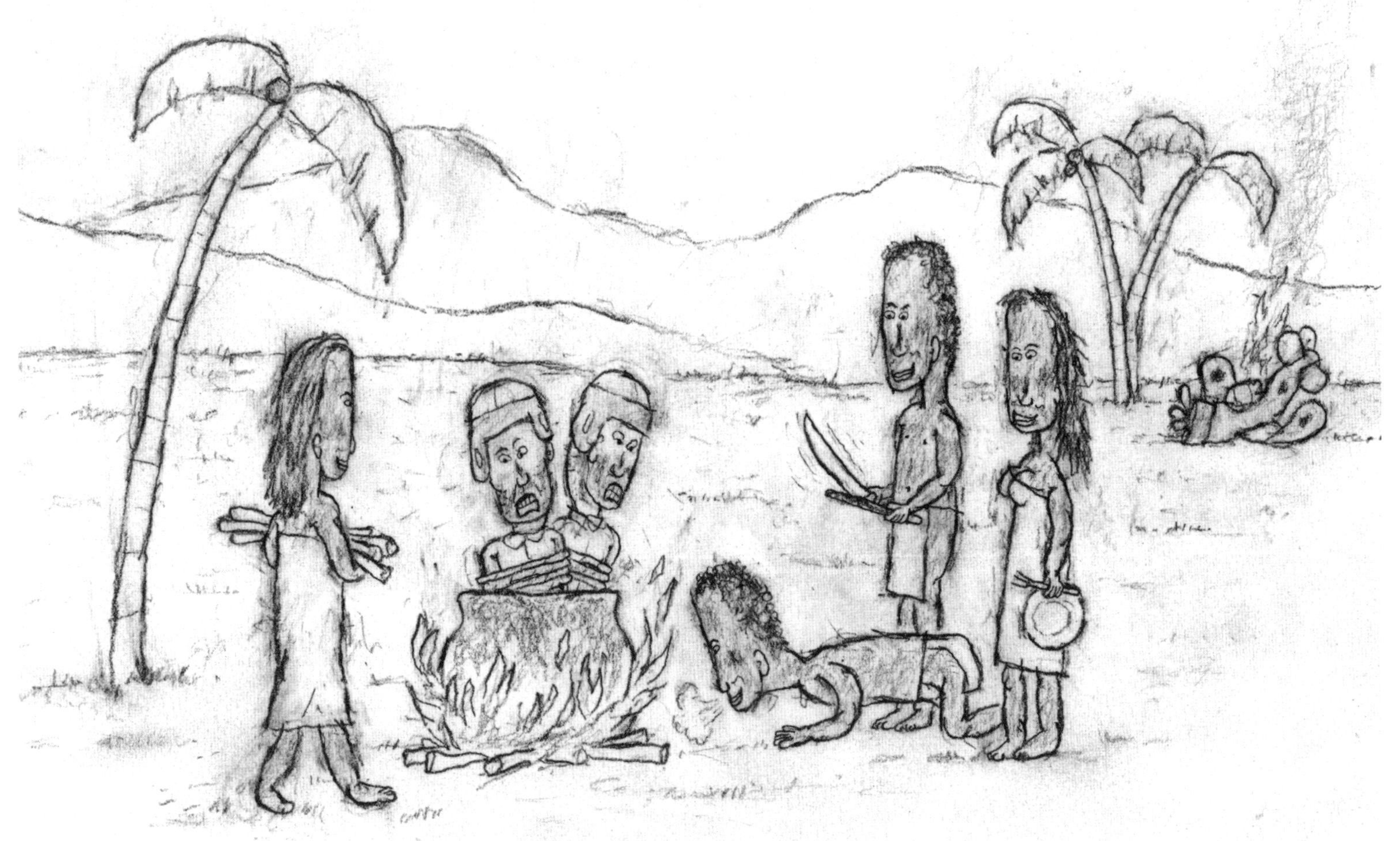
The natives never cottoned
much to the Japs.

But just like everyone else,
the natives all loved Americans.

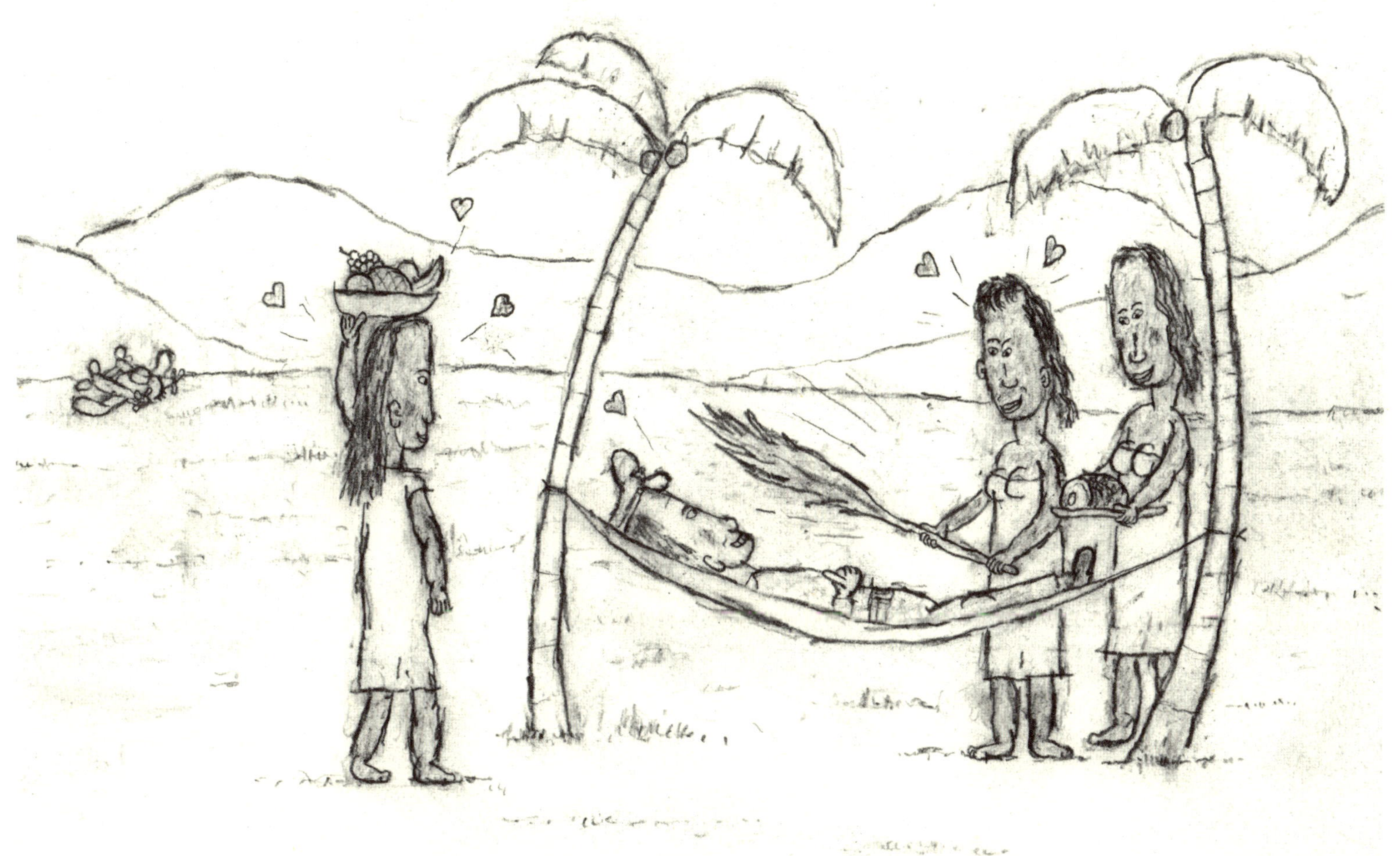

Fiendish Jap torture: the Japs would starve an
American prisoner, then put a steak dinner on the
table for him—but he'd have to step on the
American flag to get it.
(Usually our guys escaped anyway.)

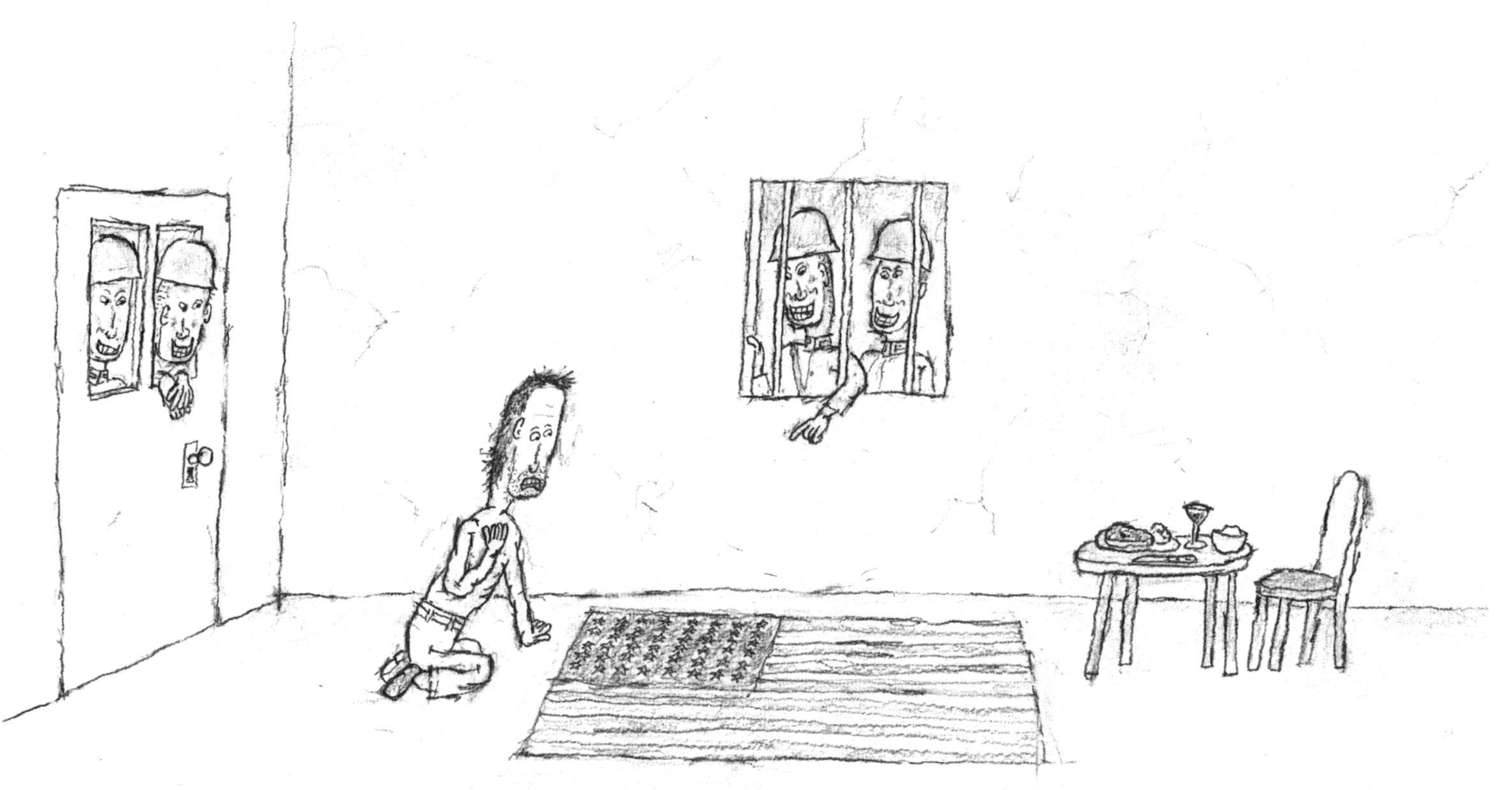

Another
torture:
Tokyo
Rose.

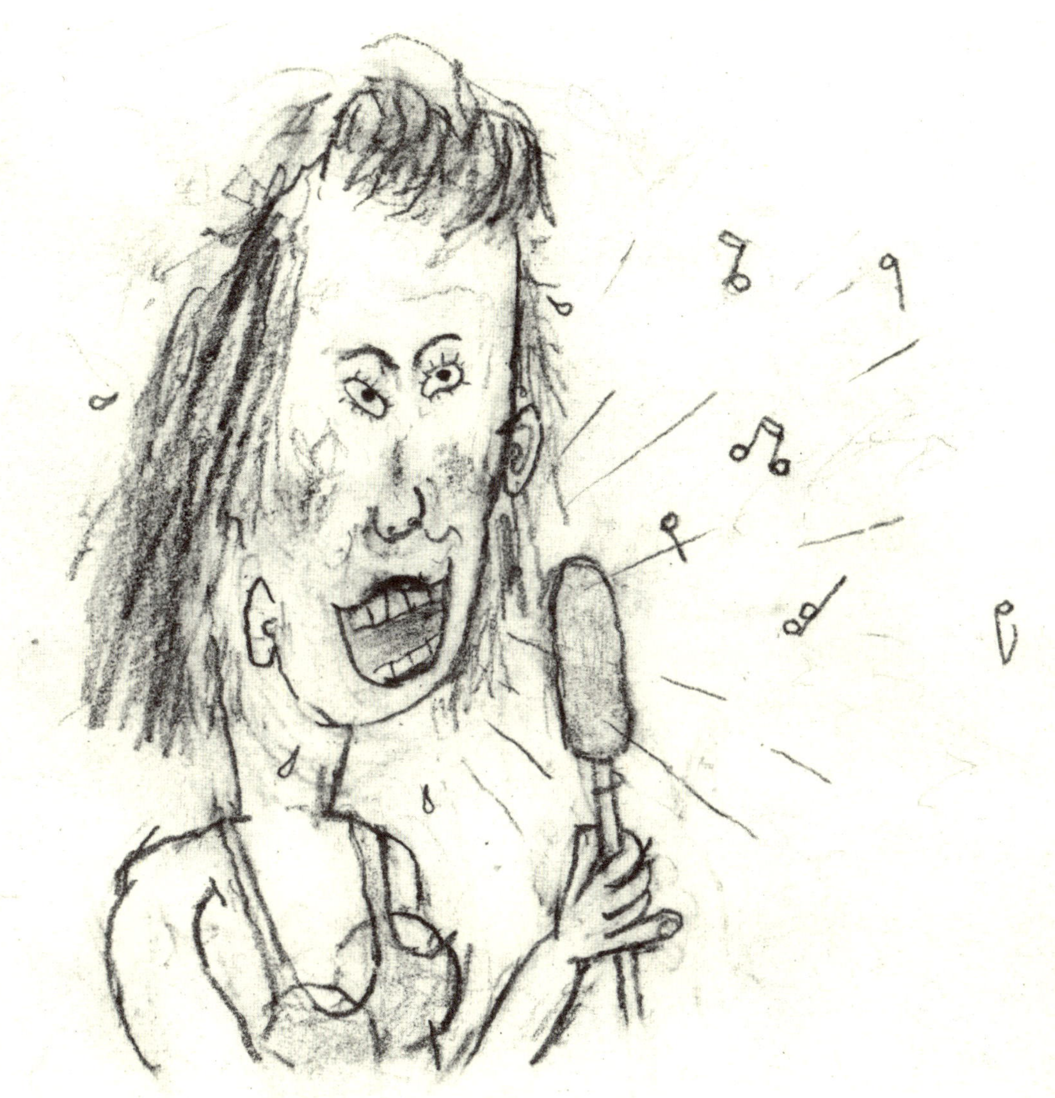

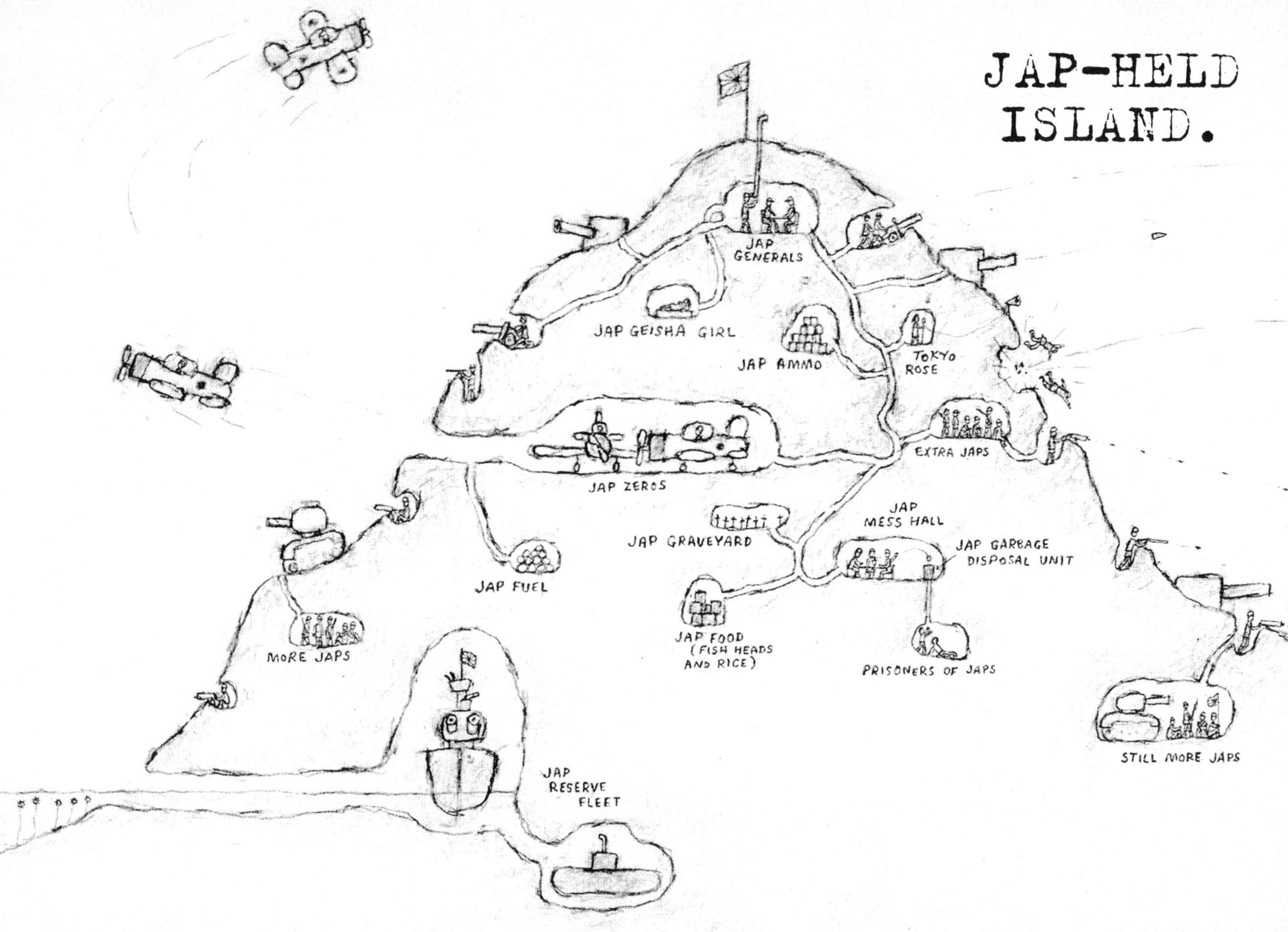

JAP-HELD ISLAND.
JAP GENERALS
JAP GEISHA GIRL
JAP AMMO
TOKYO ROSE
JAP ZEROS
EXTRA JAPS
JAP MESS HALL
JAP GRAVEYARD
JAP GARBAGE DISPOSAL UNIT
JAP FUEL
JAP FOOD
(FISH HEADS AND RICE)
PRISONERS OF JAPS
MORE JAPS
STILL MORE JAPS
JAP RESERVE FLEET

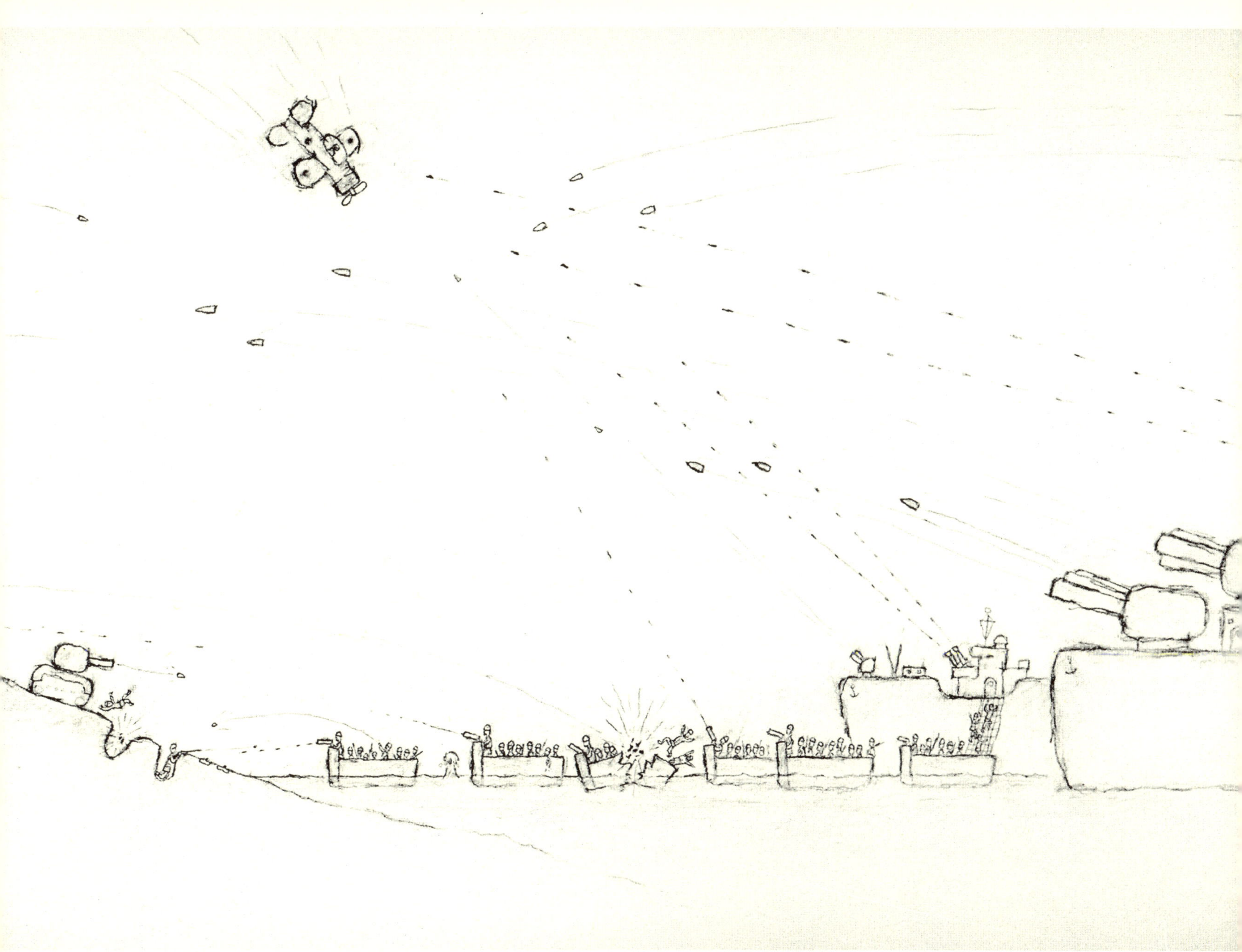

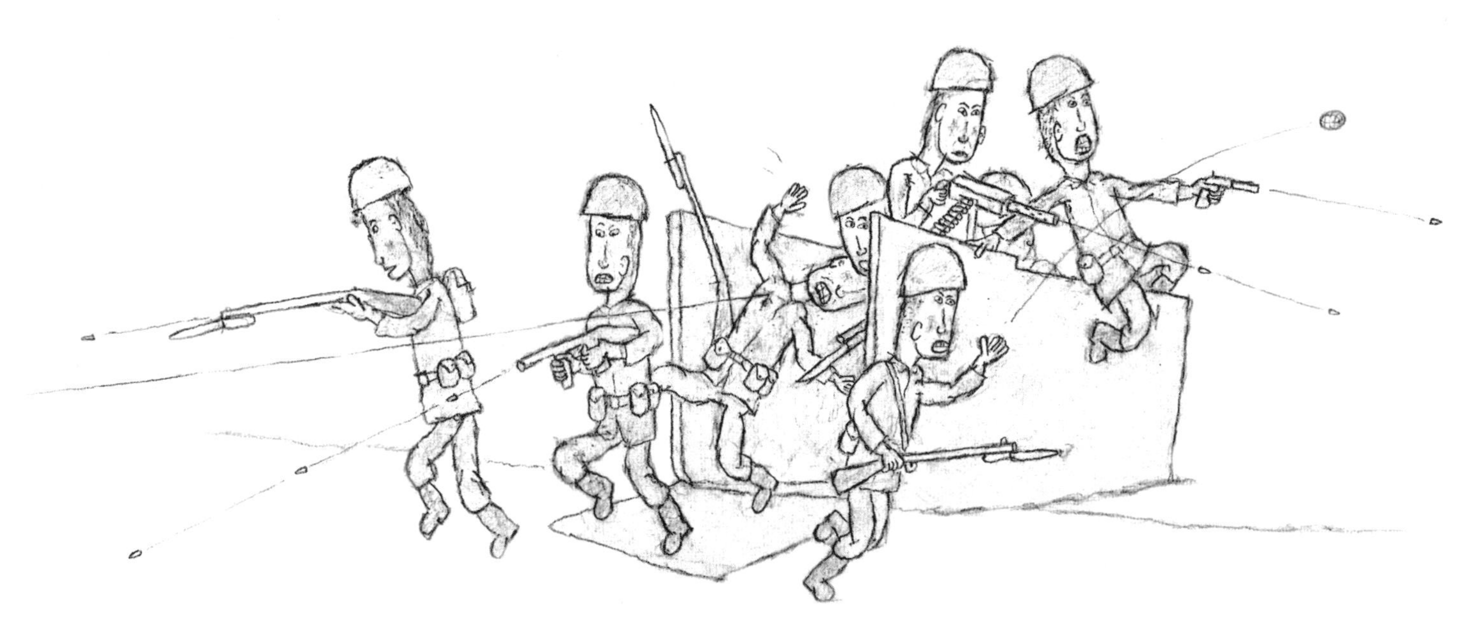

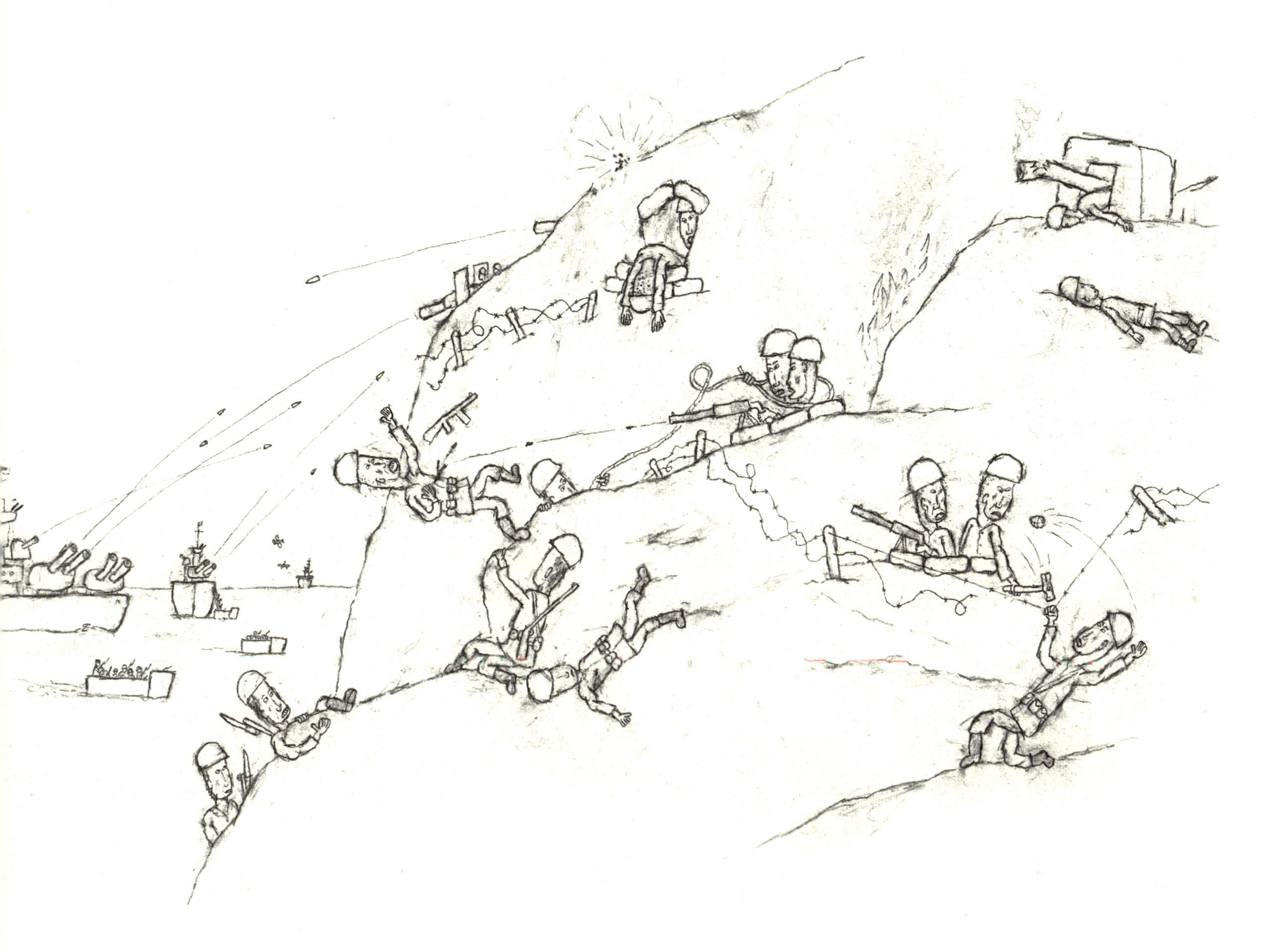

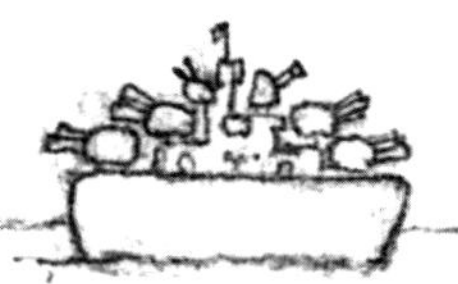

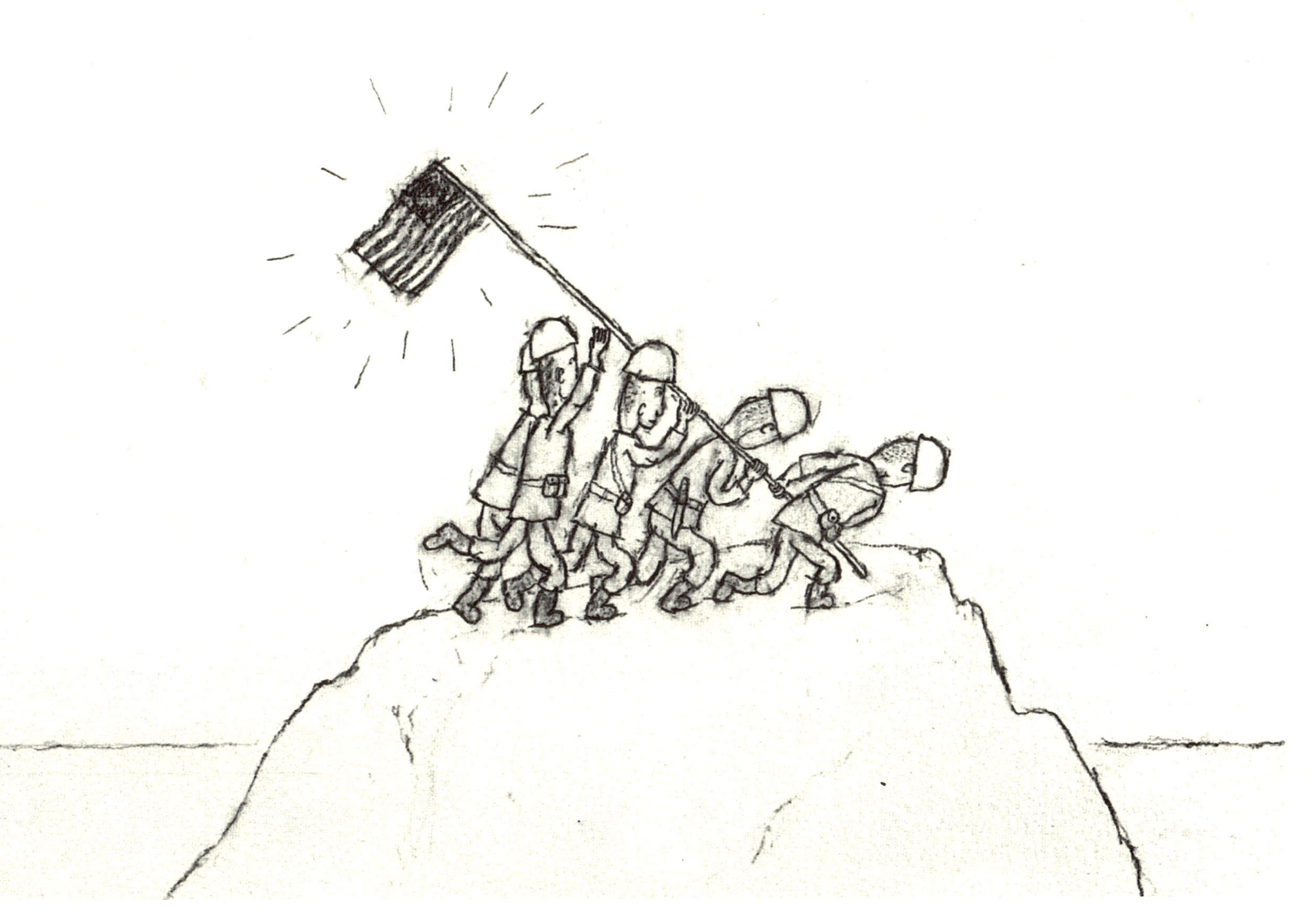

When the Jap commander saw the U.S.
flag go up, here's what he did.

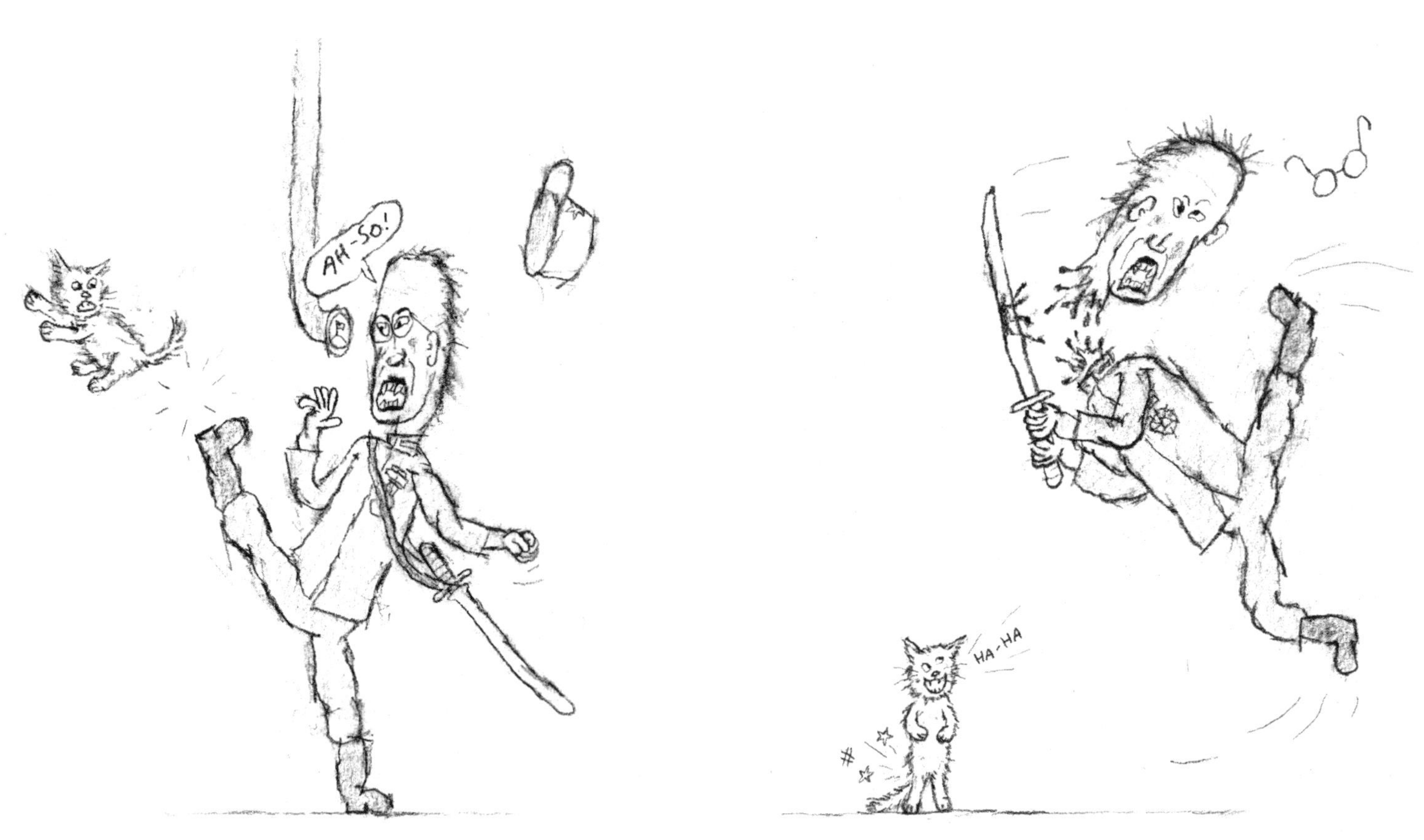

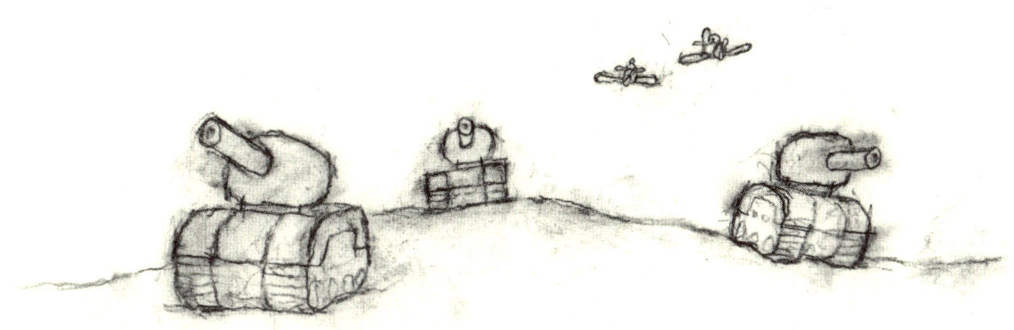

Meanwhile, the Allies had a few
surprises in store for the Huns.

This dumb fuck, General Keitel, became Commandant of the German army. He took it into his head to order his officers to join him, singing Christmas carols to Hitler.

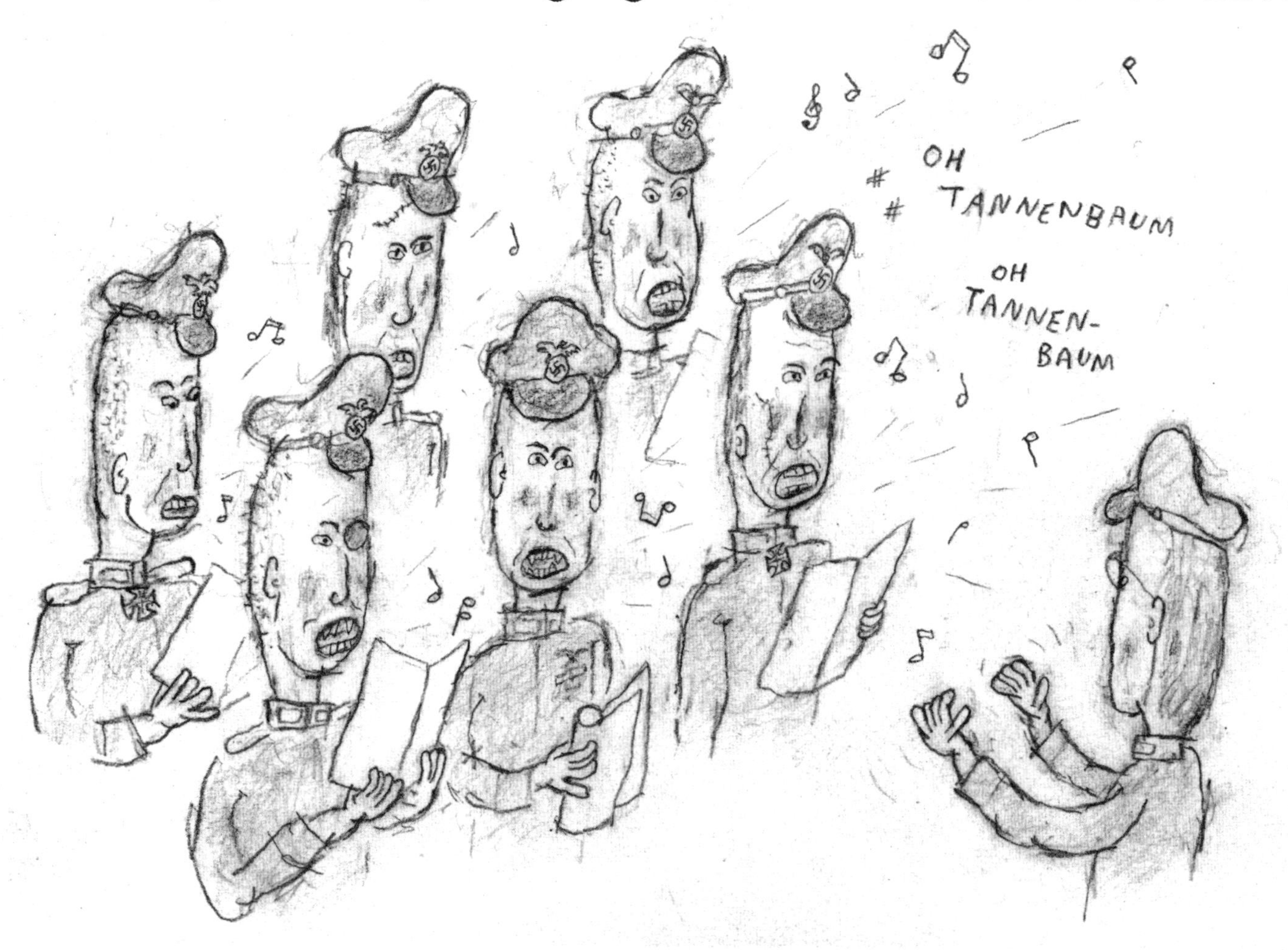

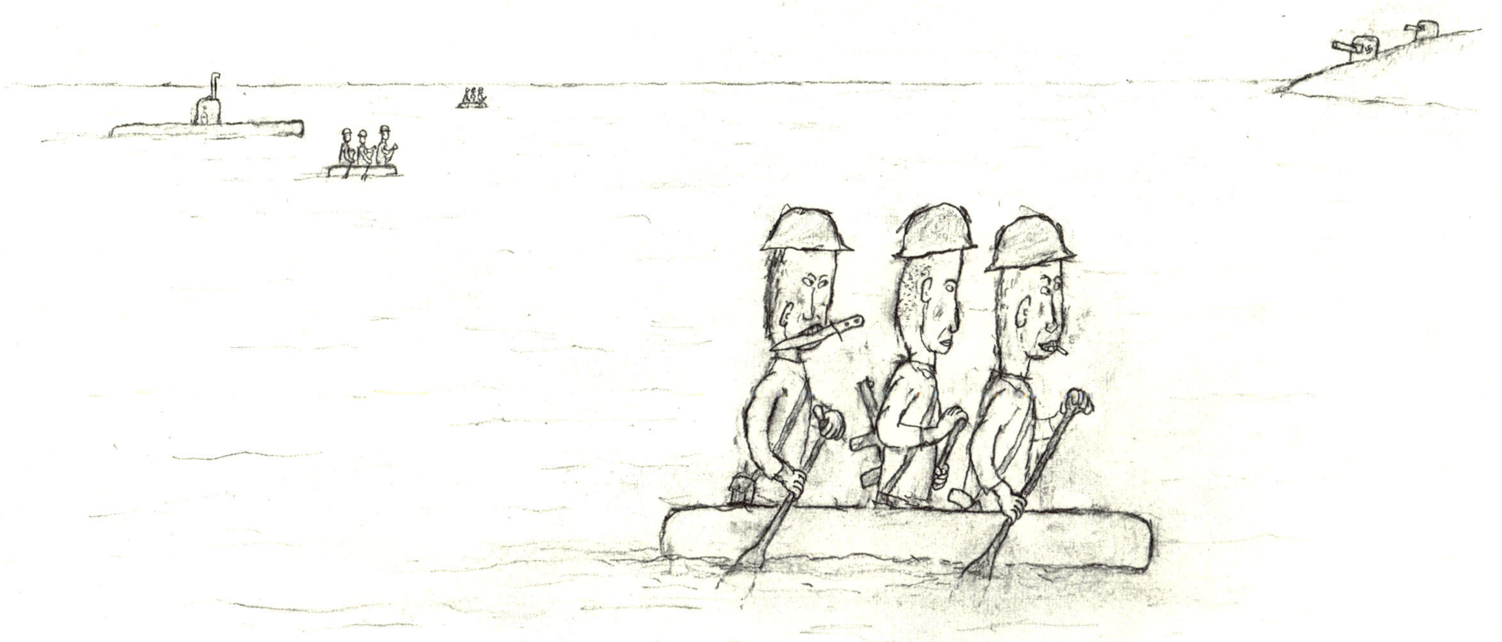

Tommy commandos at work.

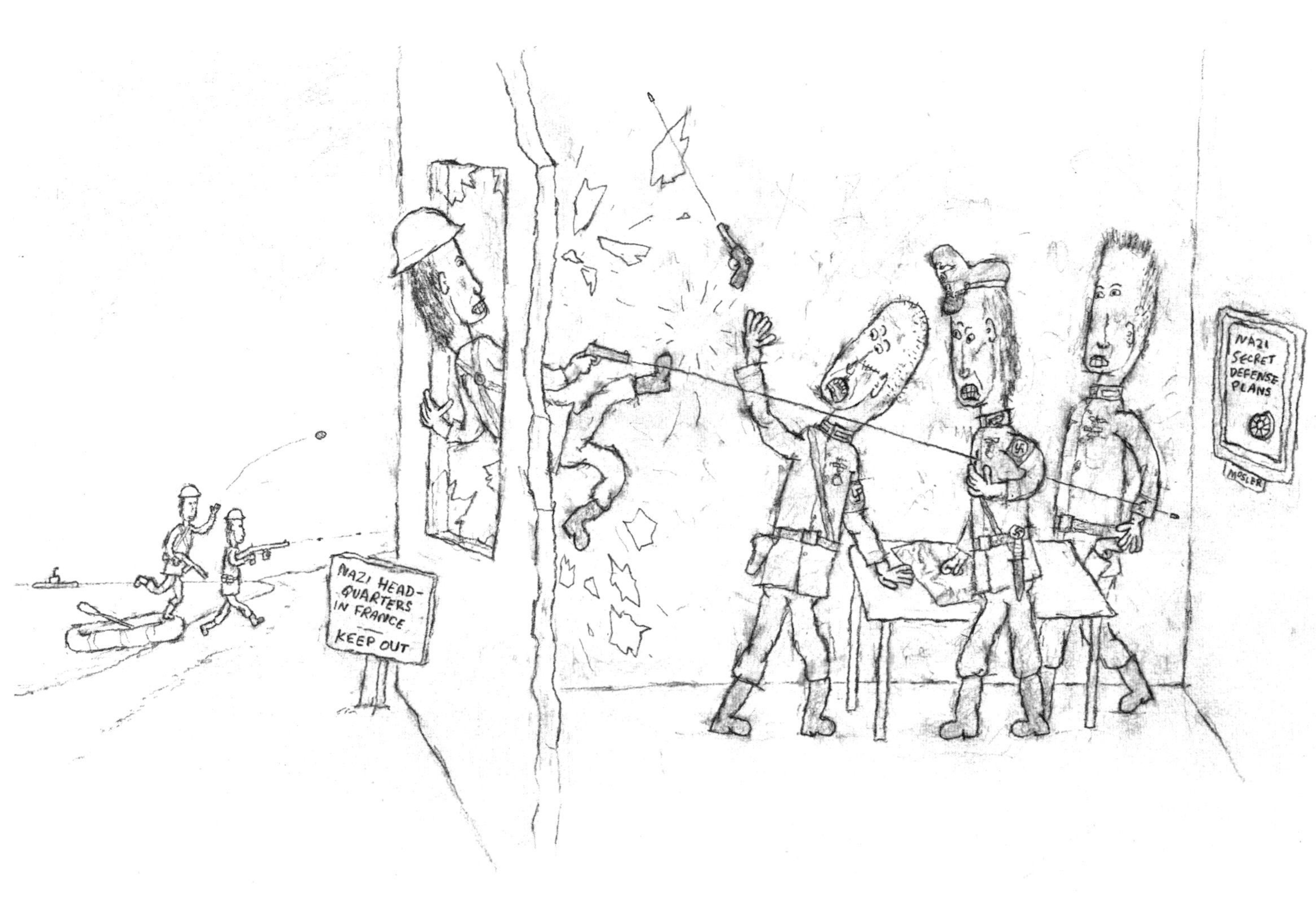

NAZI HEAD-
QUARTERS
IN FRANCE
KEEP OUT
NAZI
SECRET
DEFENSE
PLANS
MOSLER

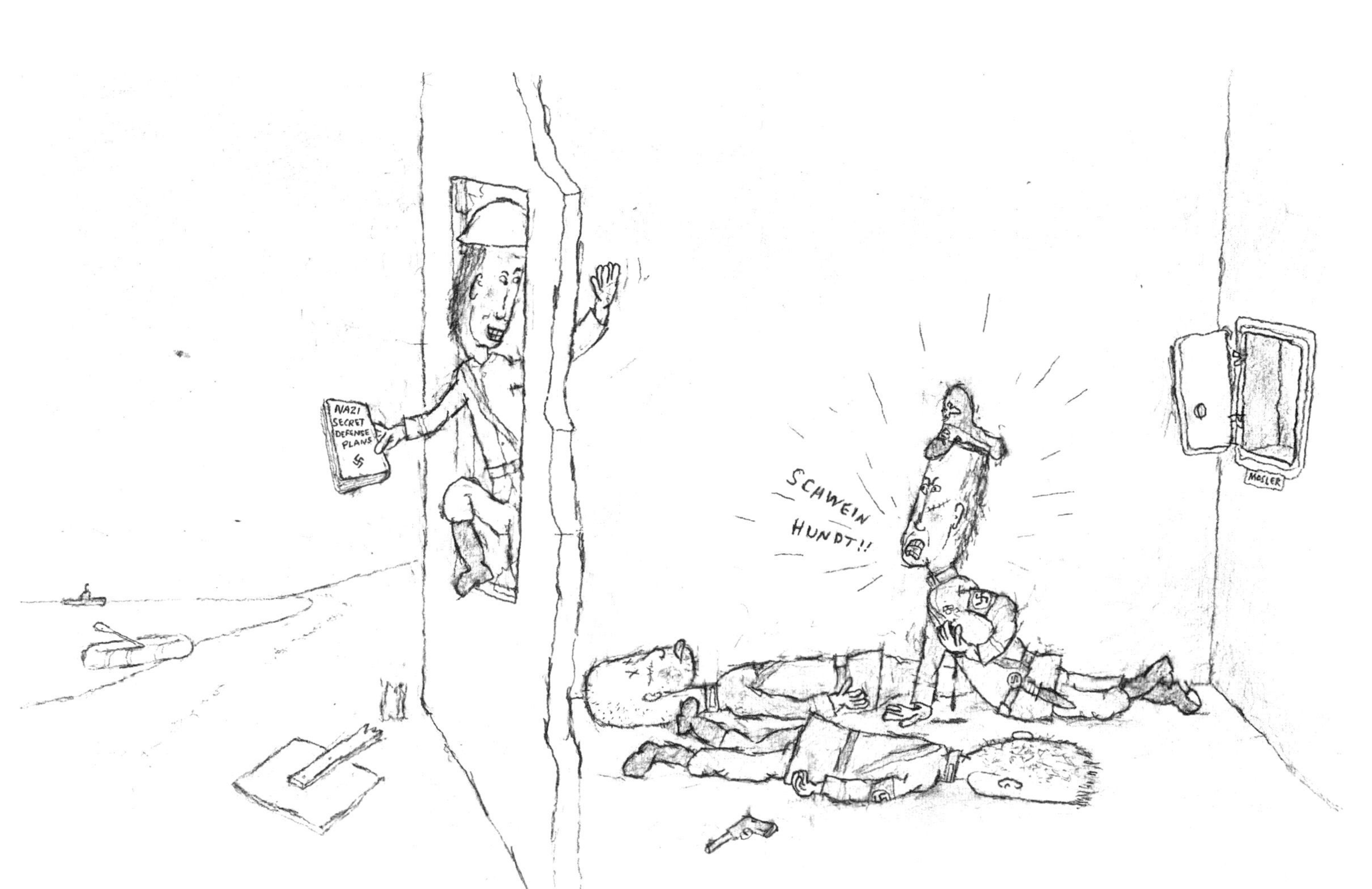

NAZI SECRET DEFENSE PLANS
SCHWEIN HUNDT!!
MOSLER

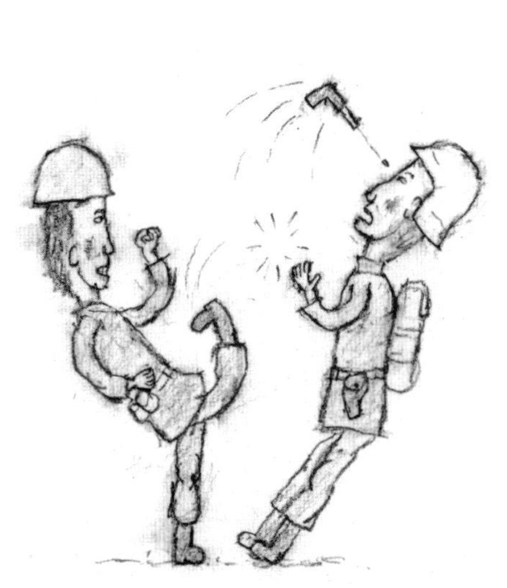

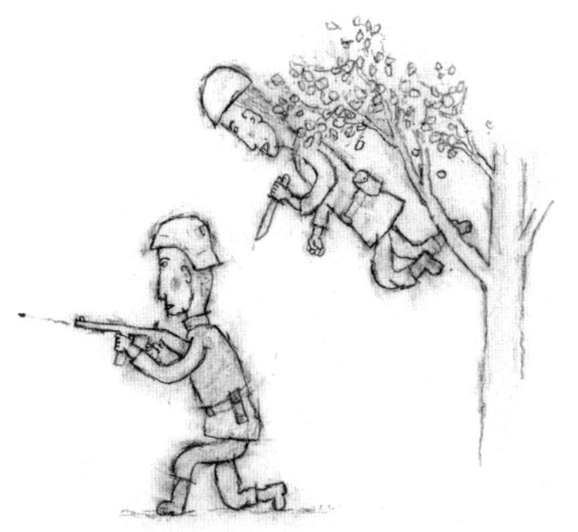

Sometimes our
side ran out
of ammo.

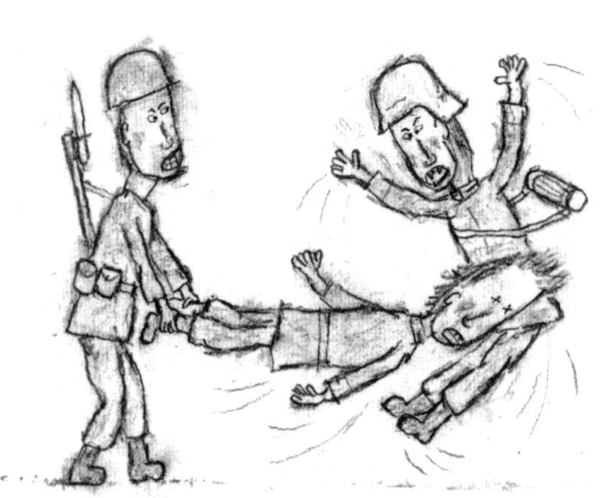

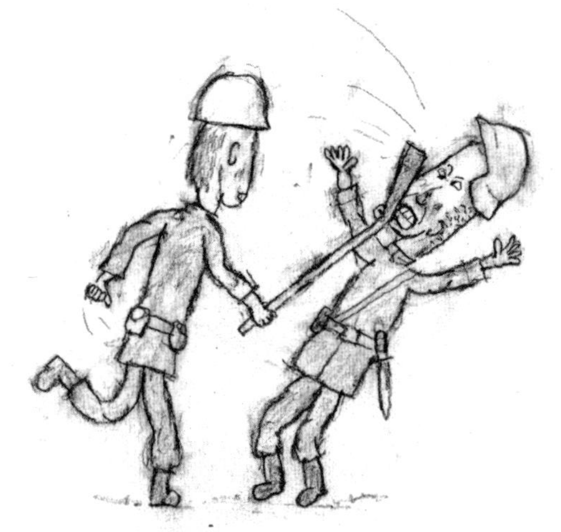

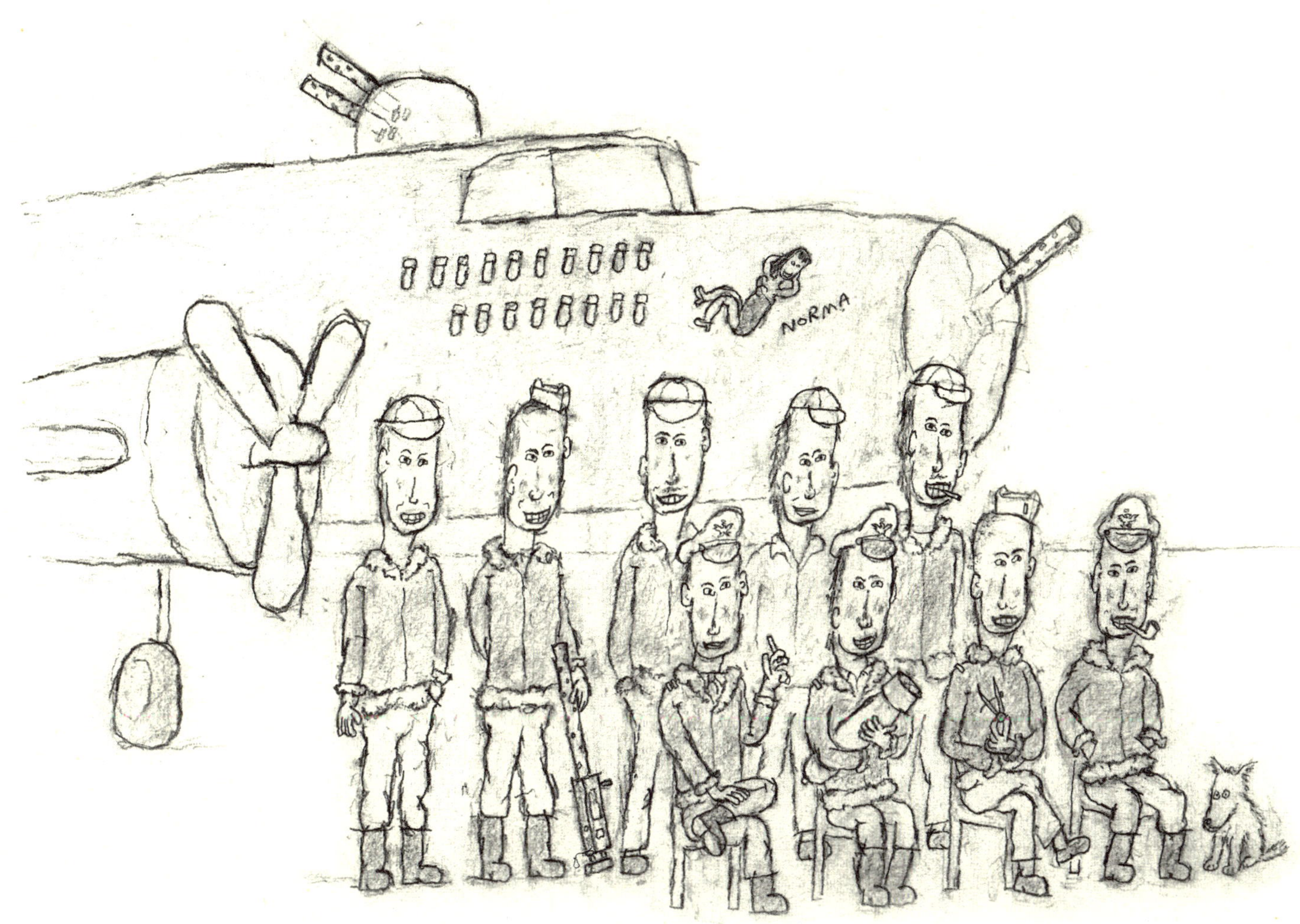

NORMA

The pilot and the co-pilot
got to drive the plane.

The bombadier got
to drop the bombs.

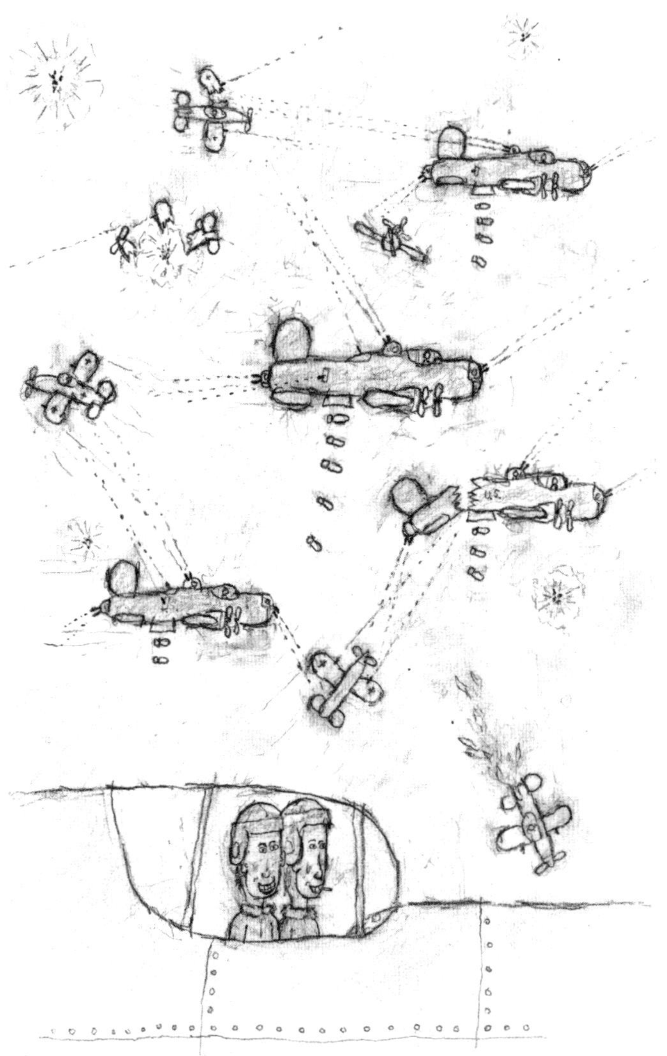

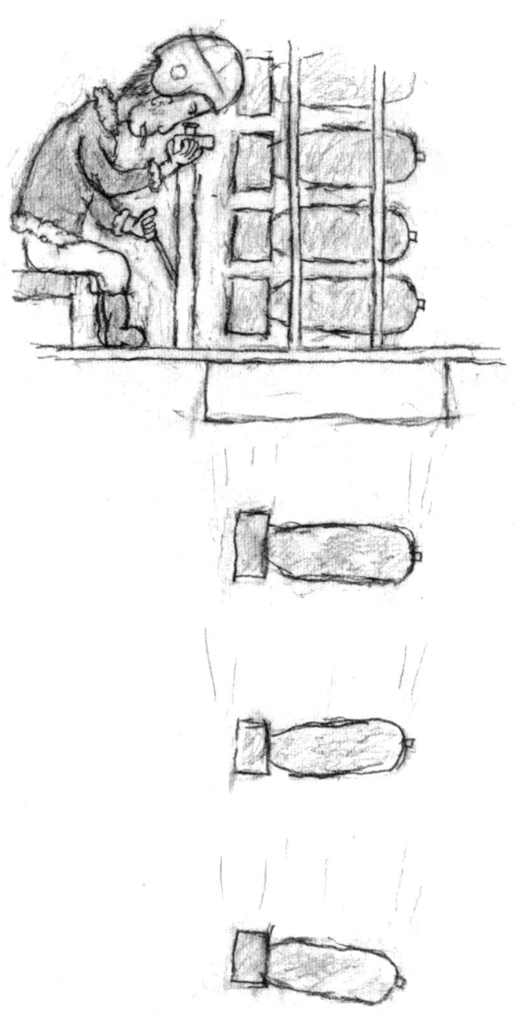

But being tail gunner
was most fun of all.

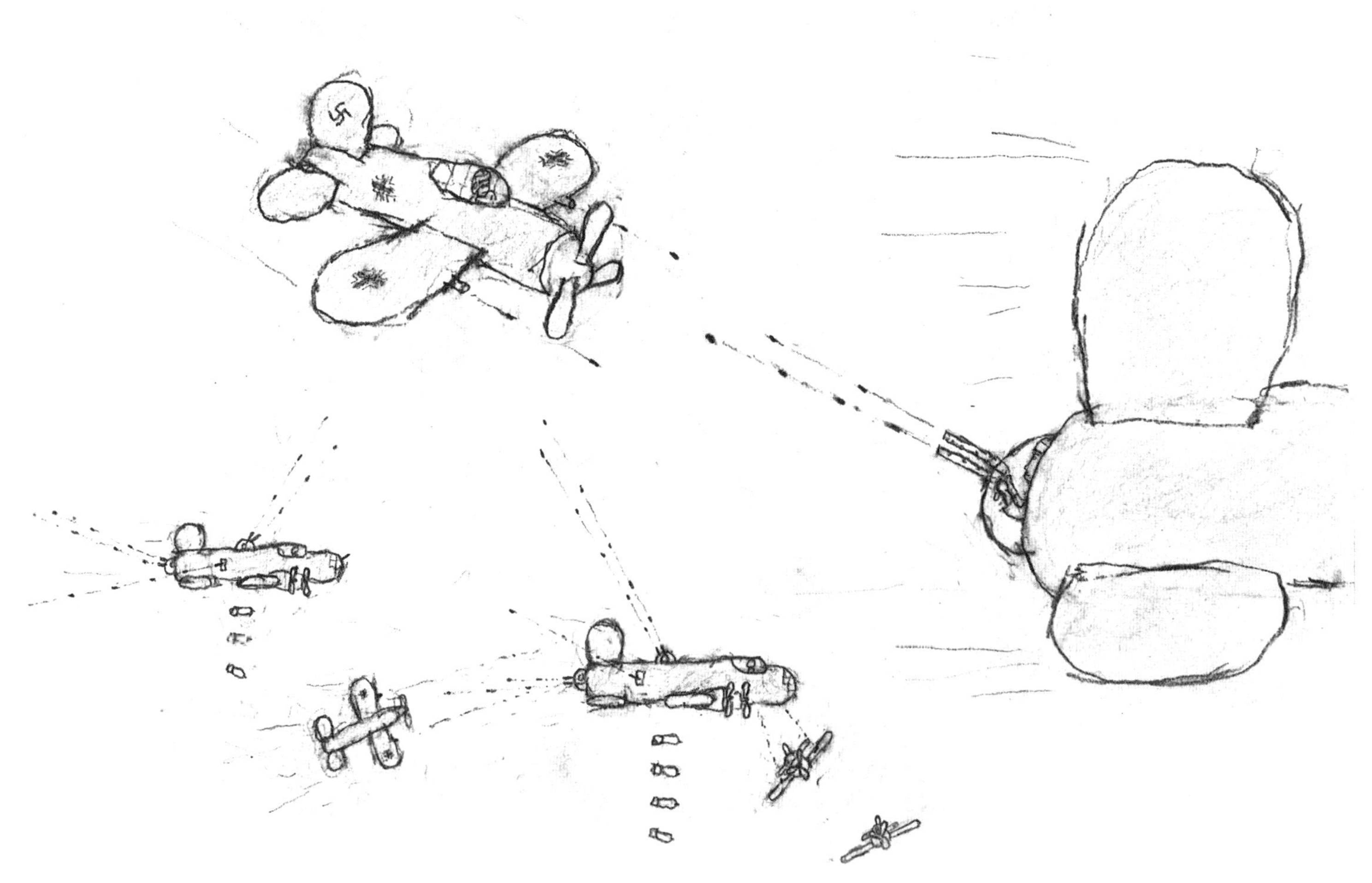

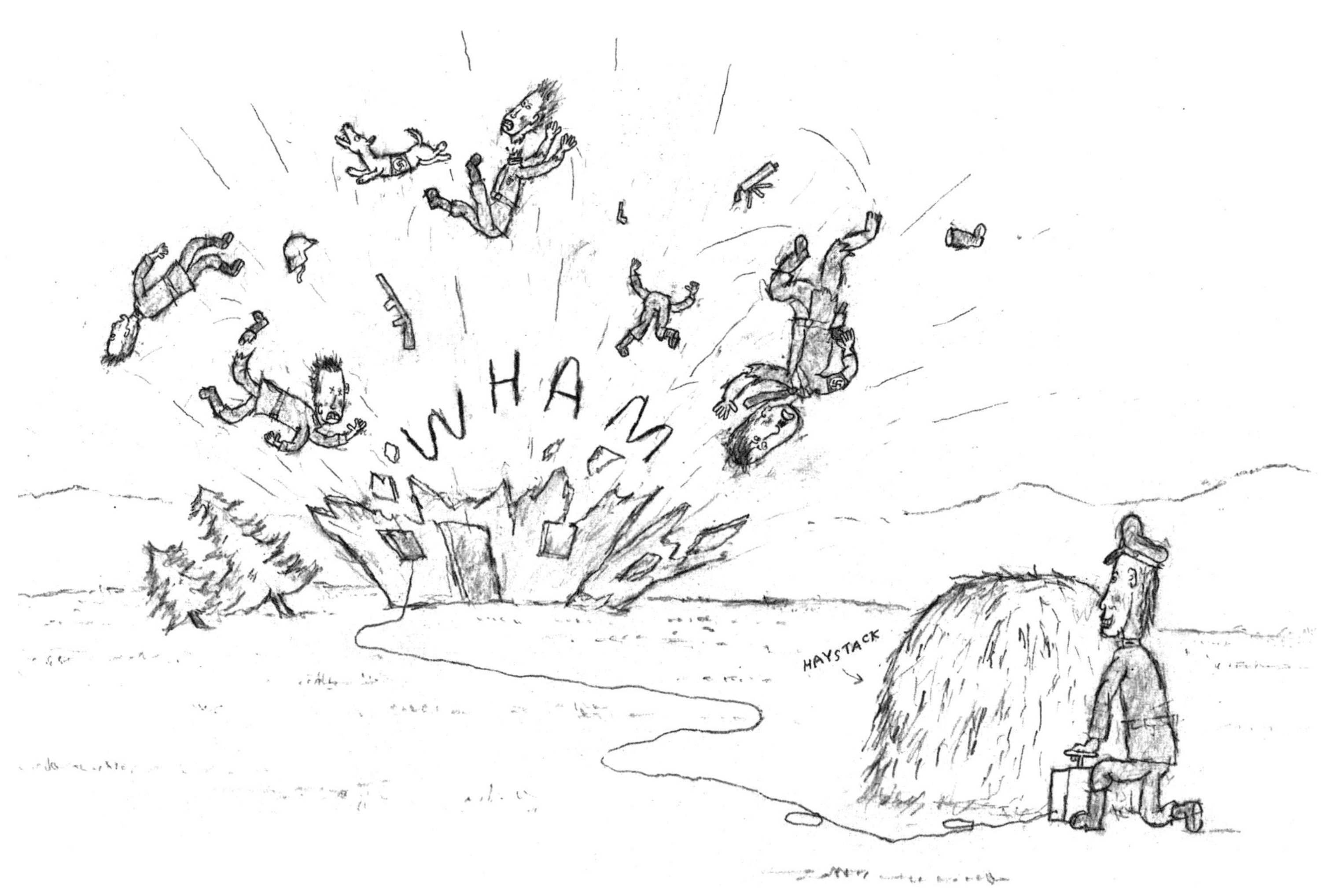

There were a few good Germans. They
tried to blow up Hitler.

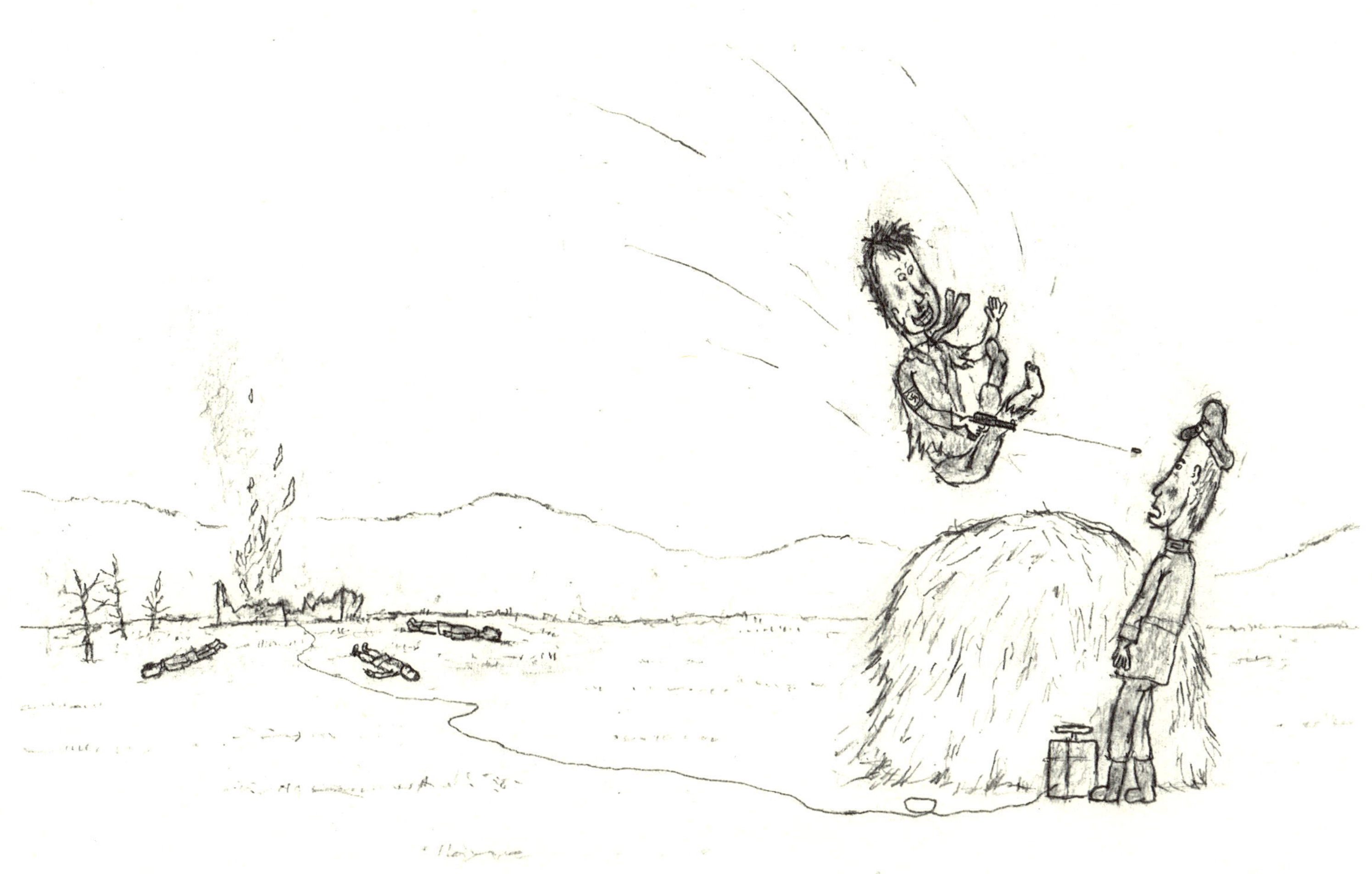

But Hitler had nine lives, like a cat. (The good
Japs would have tried to blow up Tojo except for
one thing—there weren't any good Japs.)

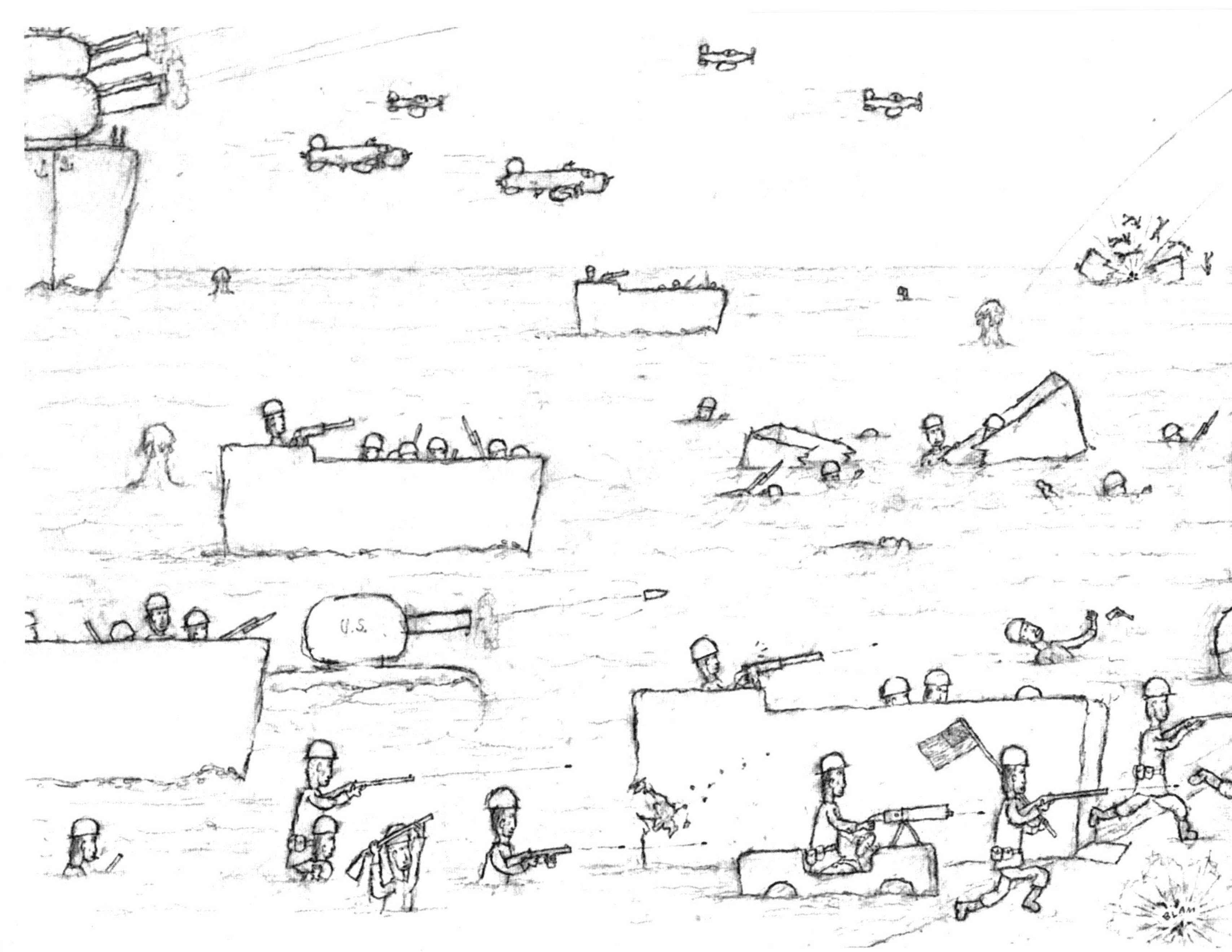

U.S.
BLAM

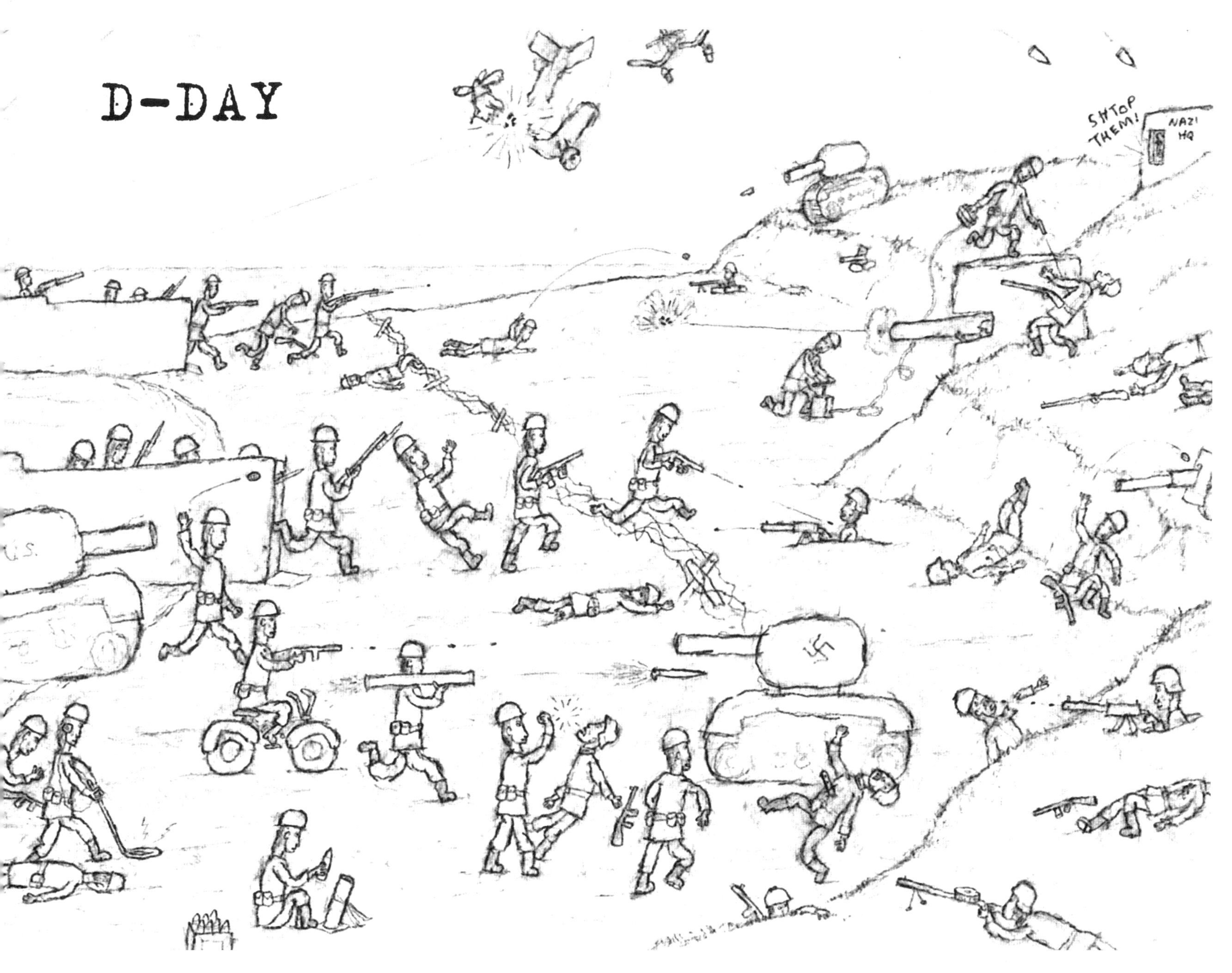

D-DAY
SHTOP THEM!
NAZI HQ
U.S.

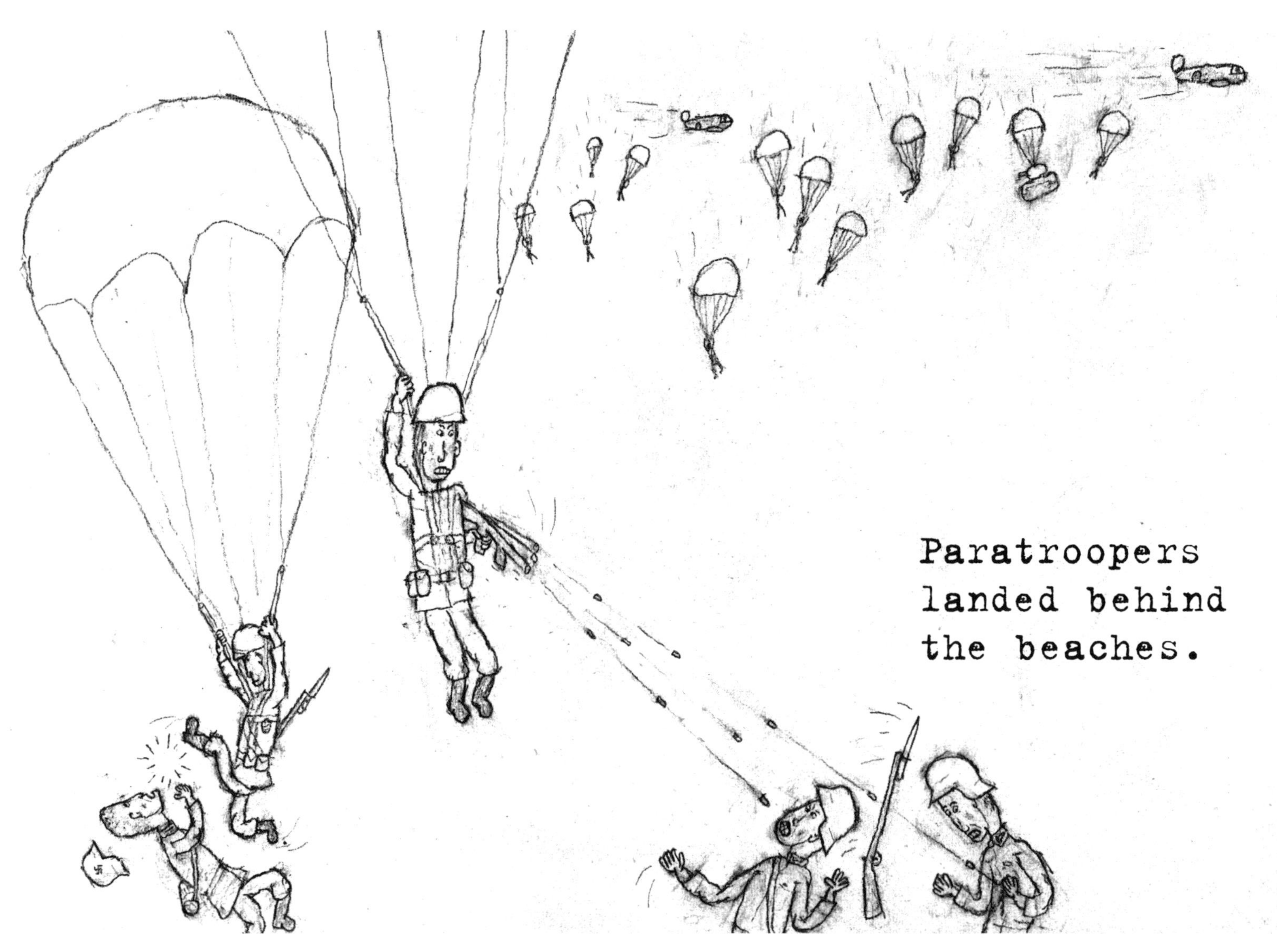

Paratroopers
landed behind
the beaches.

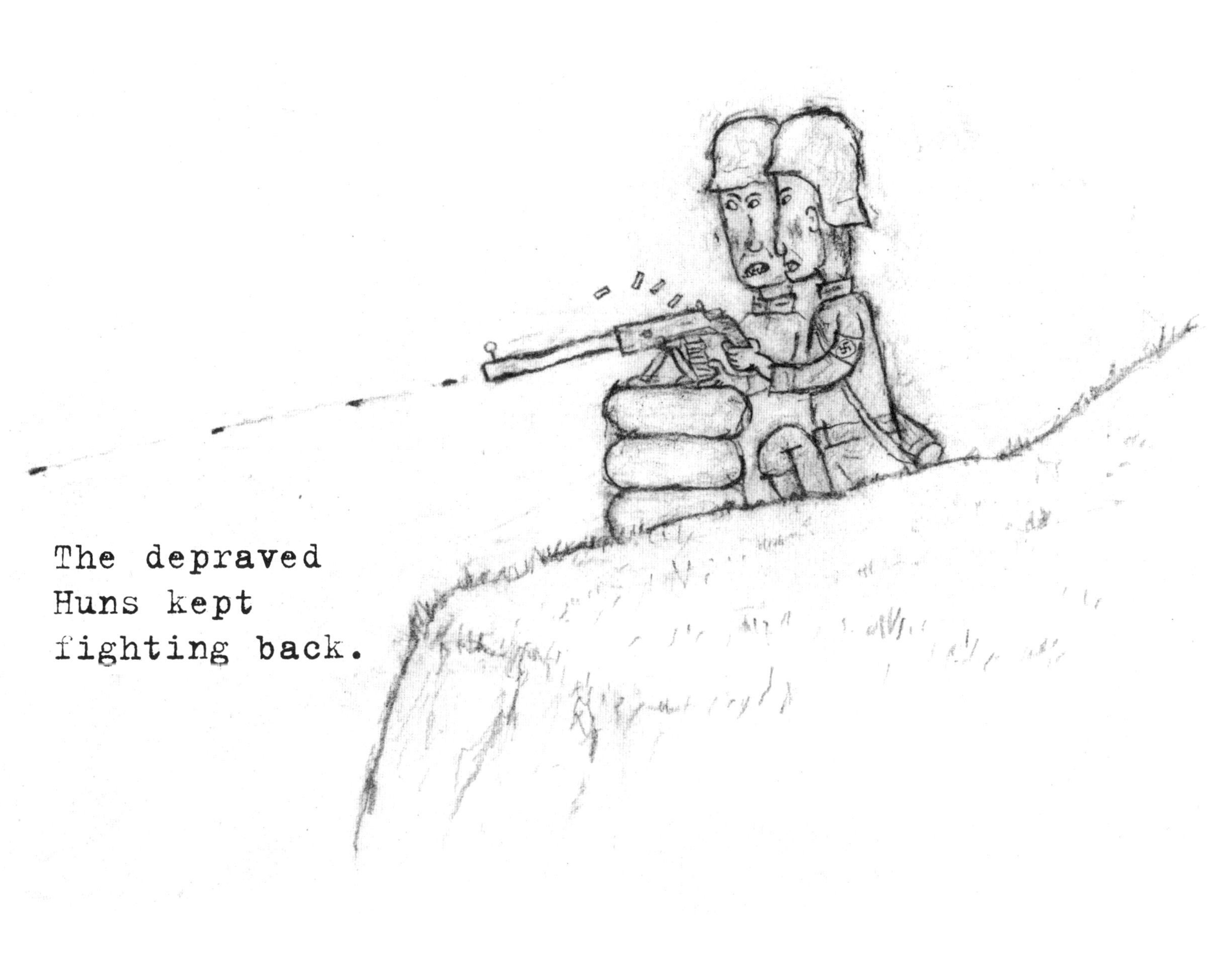

The depraved
Huns kept
fighting back.

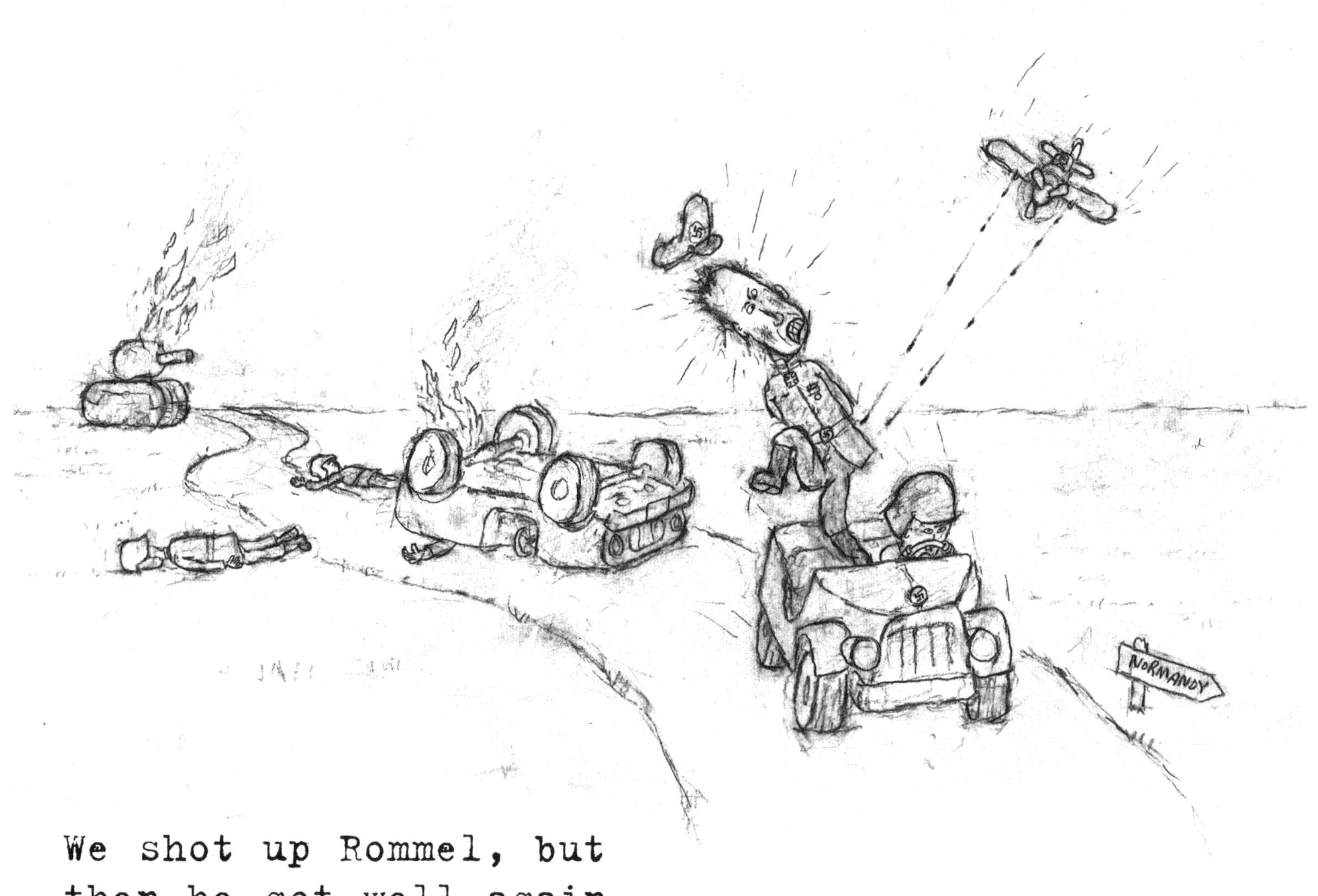

We shot up Rommel, but
then he got well again.

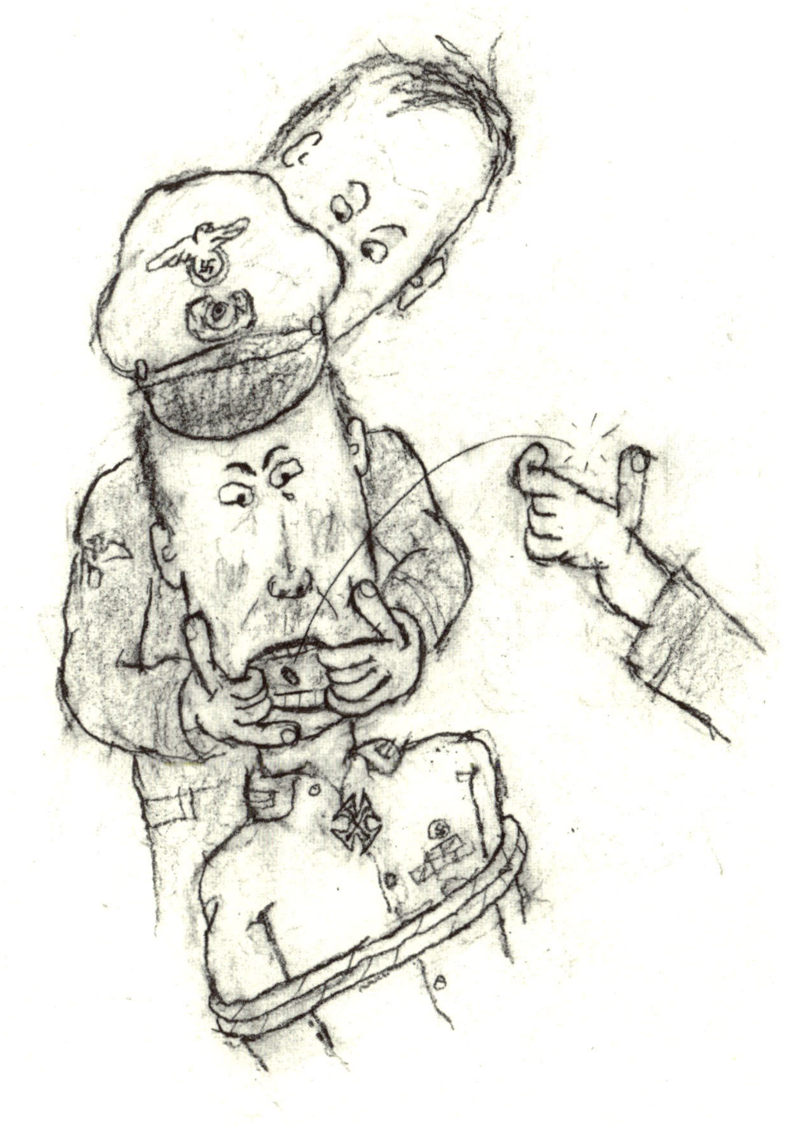

Later, Hitler
was so jealous
of Rommel that
he had his
henchmen give
Rommel a poison
pill.

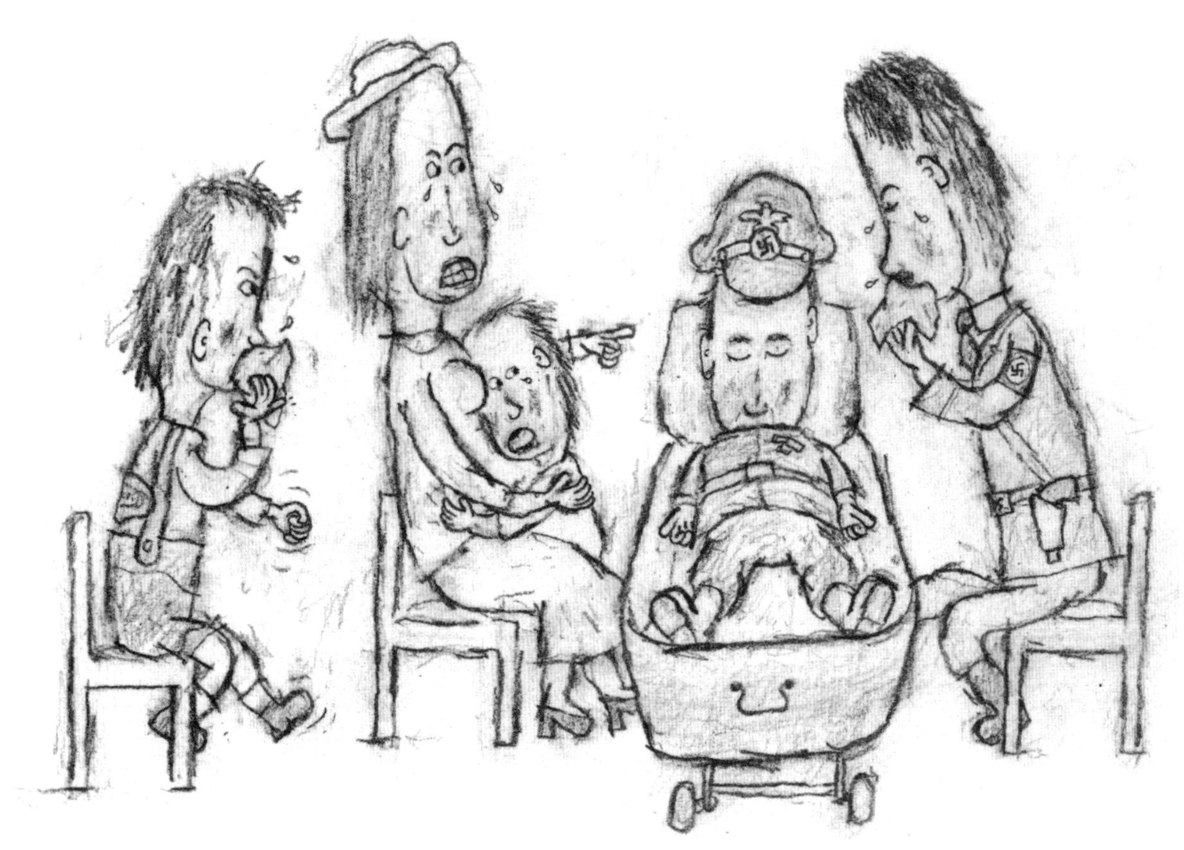

Then Hitler had the crust to go and cry
phony crocodile tears at Rommel's funeral.

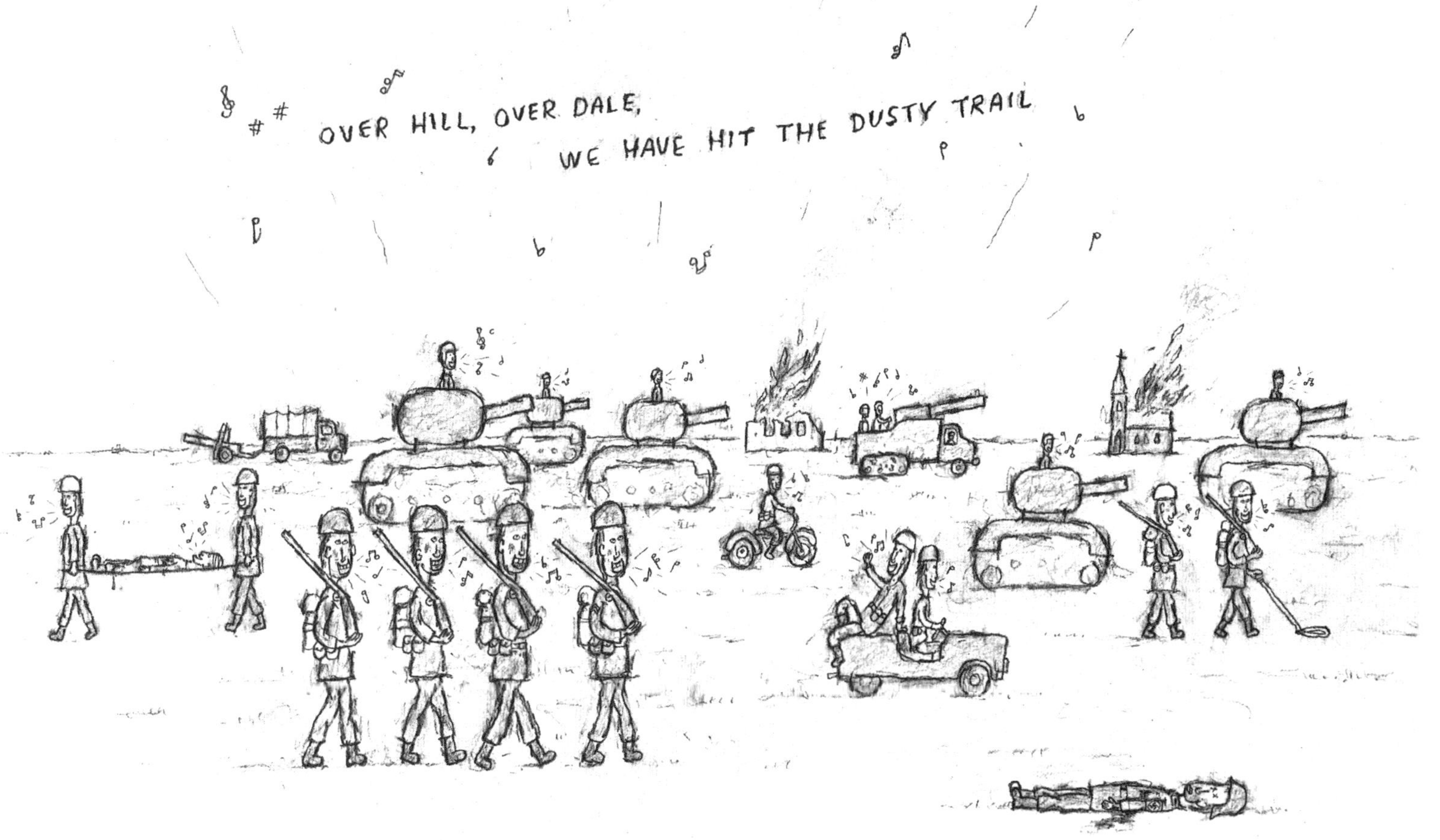

Our guys liked to sing.

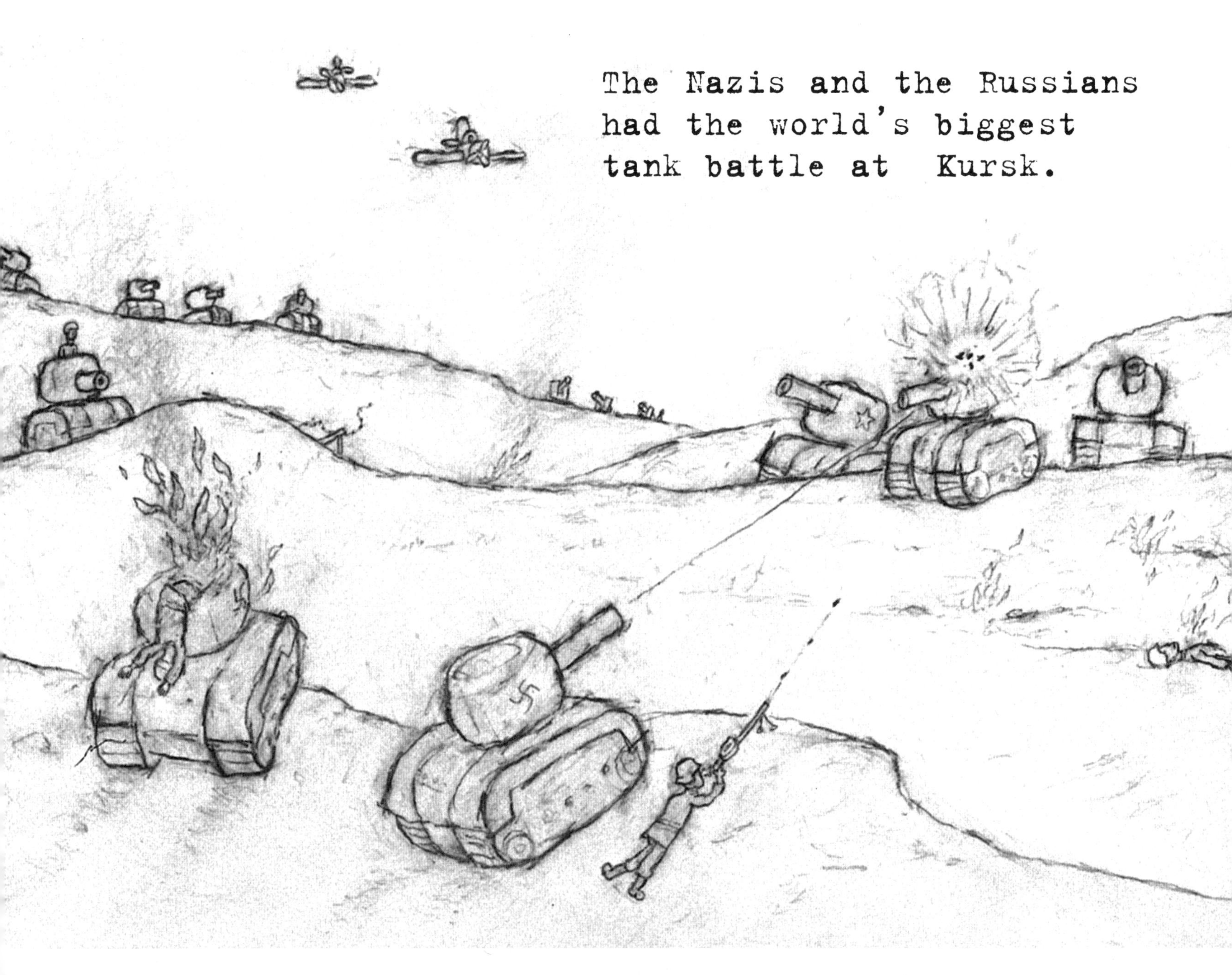
The Nazis and the Russians
had the world's biggest
tank battle at Kursk.

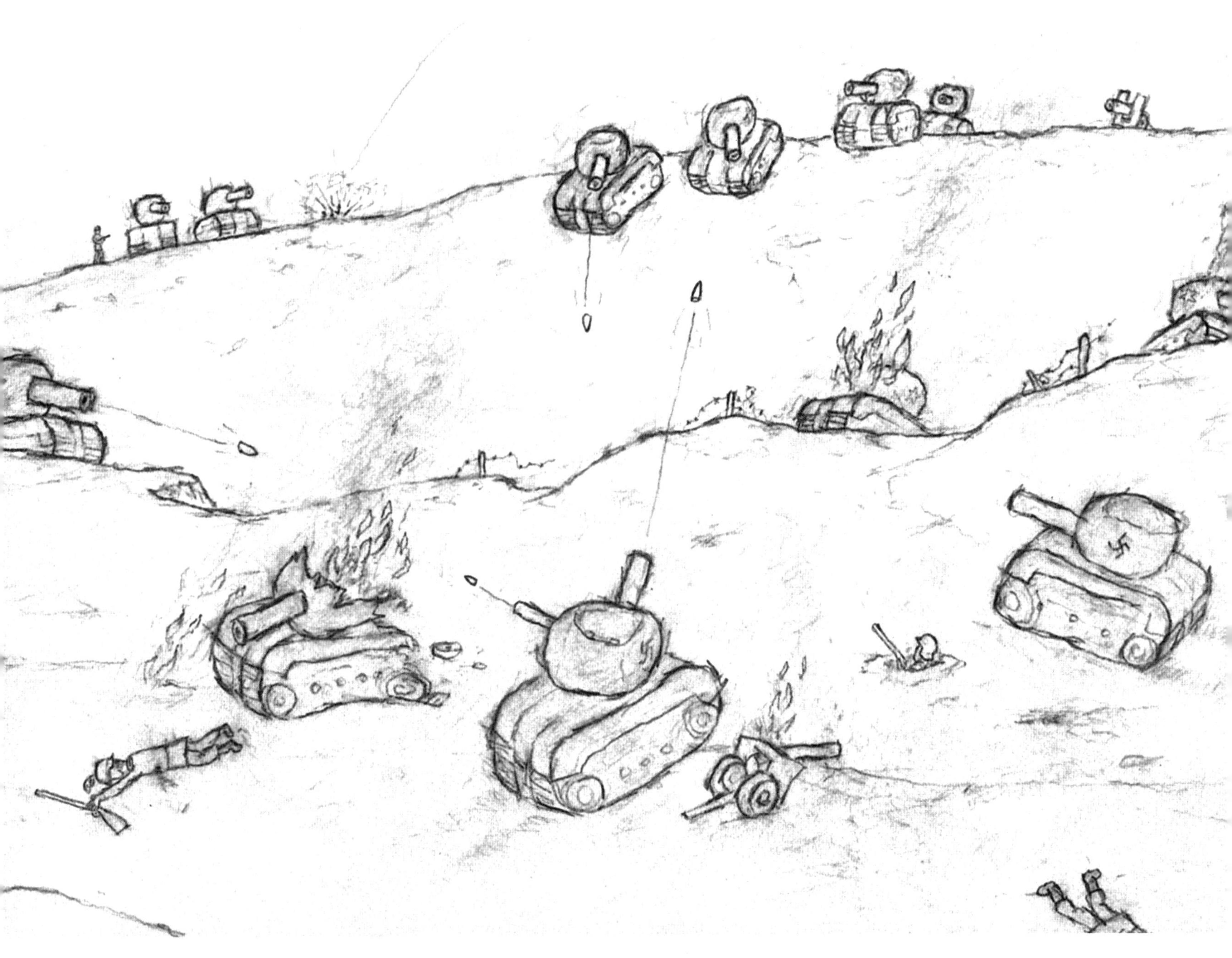

Here's how we used jujitsu.

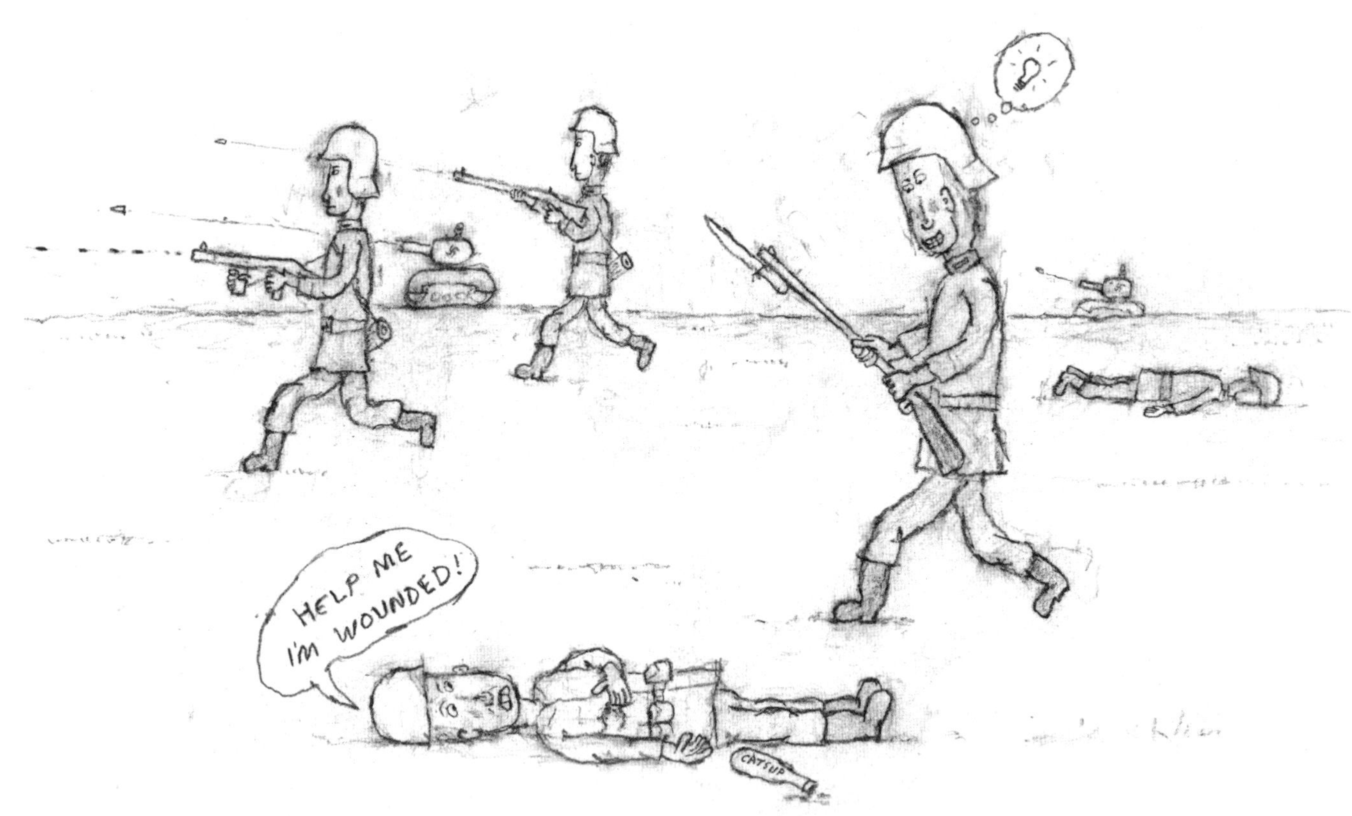

1.
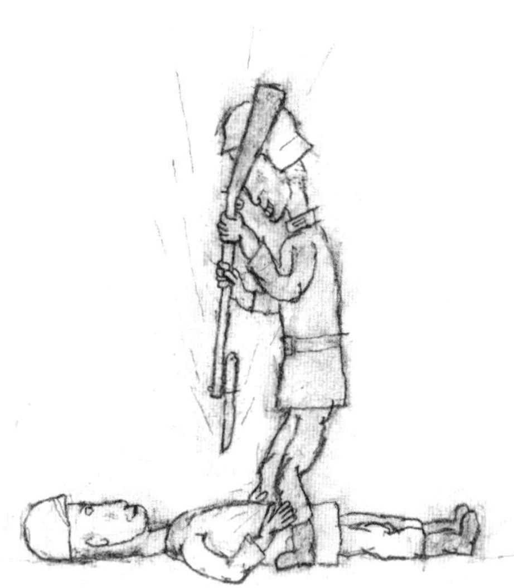

2.
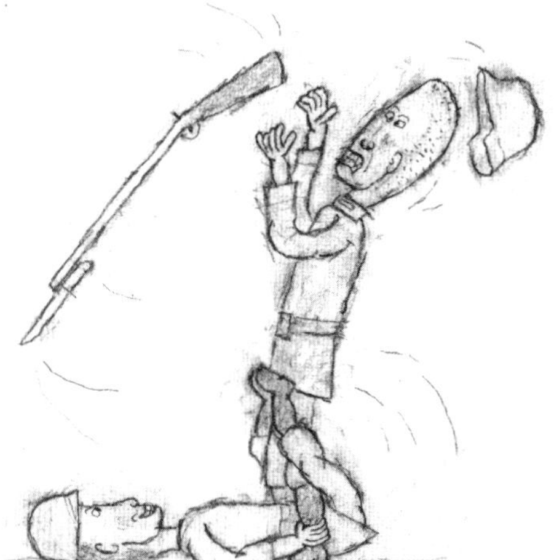

3.
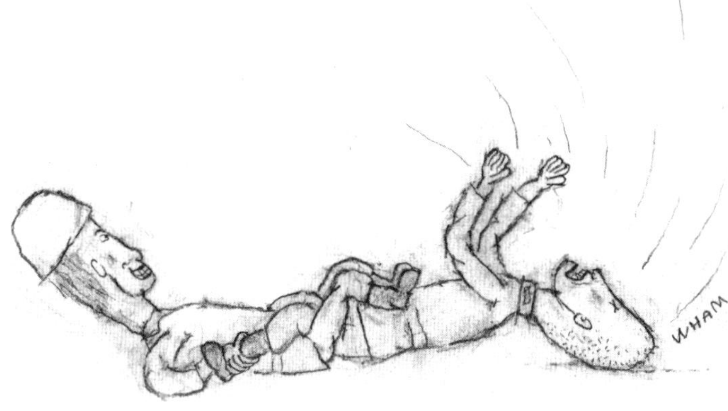
WHAM

Then, in Belgium the Krauts brought up some
divisions from the rear for a last-ditch
battle at the Bulge. As usual, they lost.

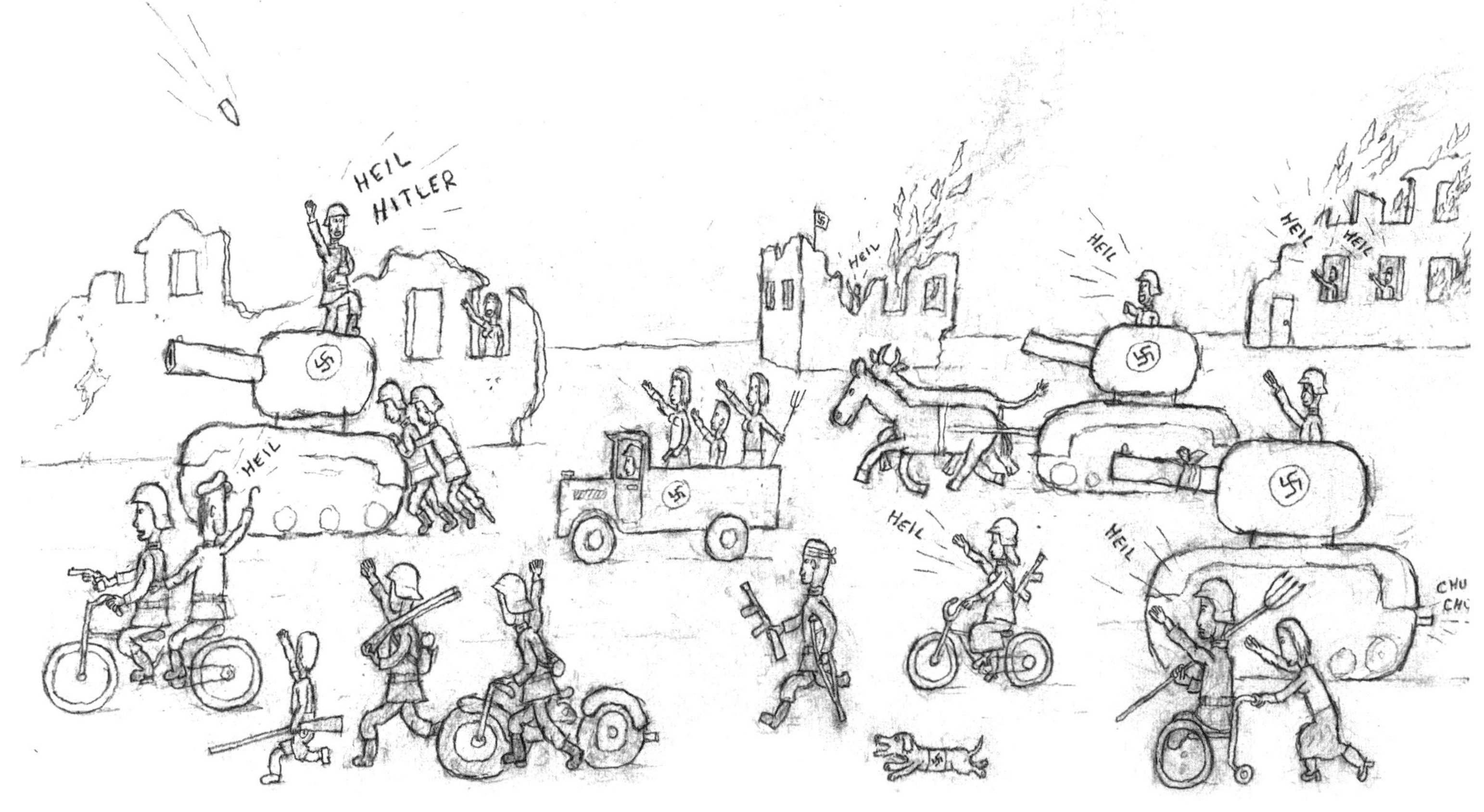

When the dumb Kraut General asked
the Americans to surrender, here's
what he got told.

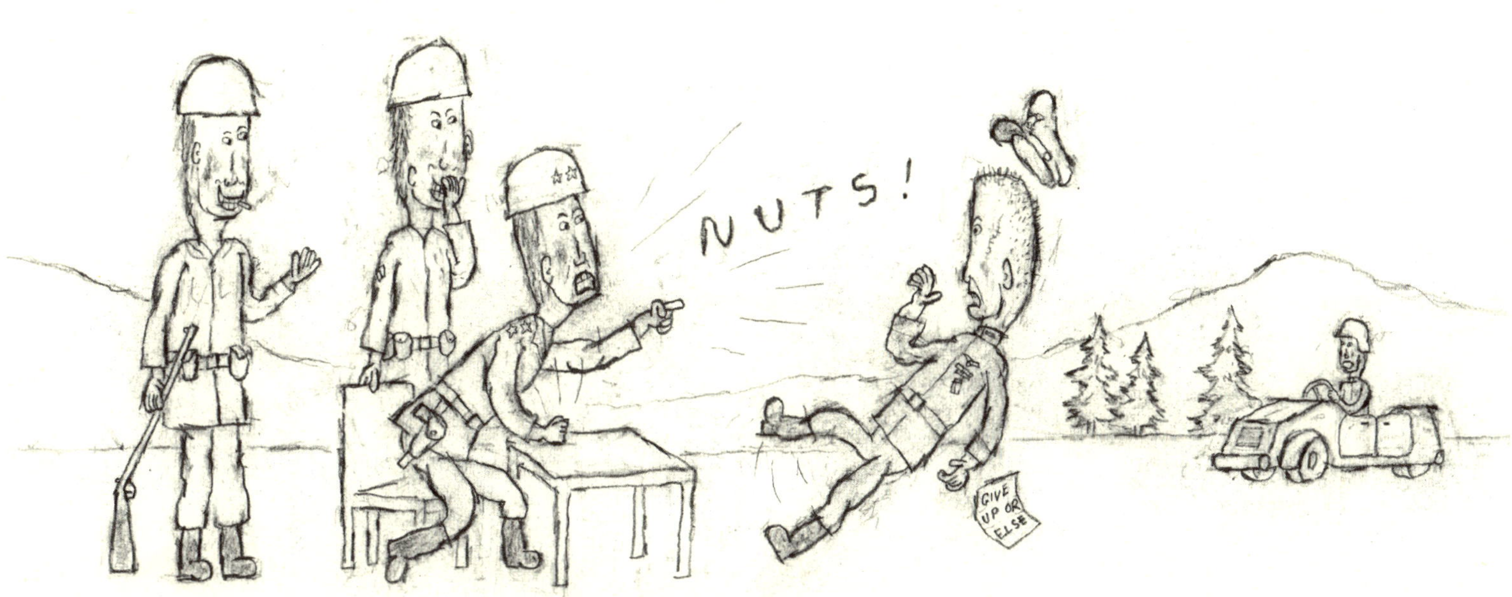

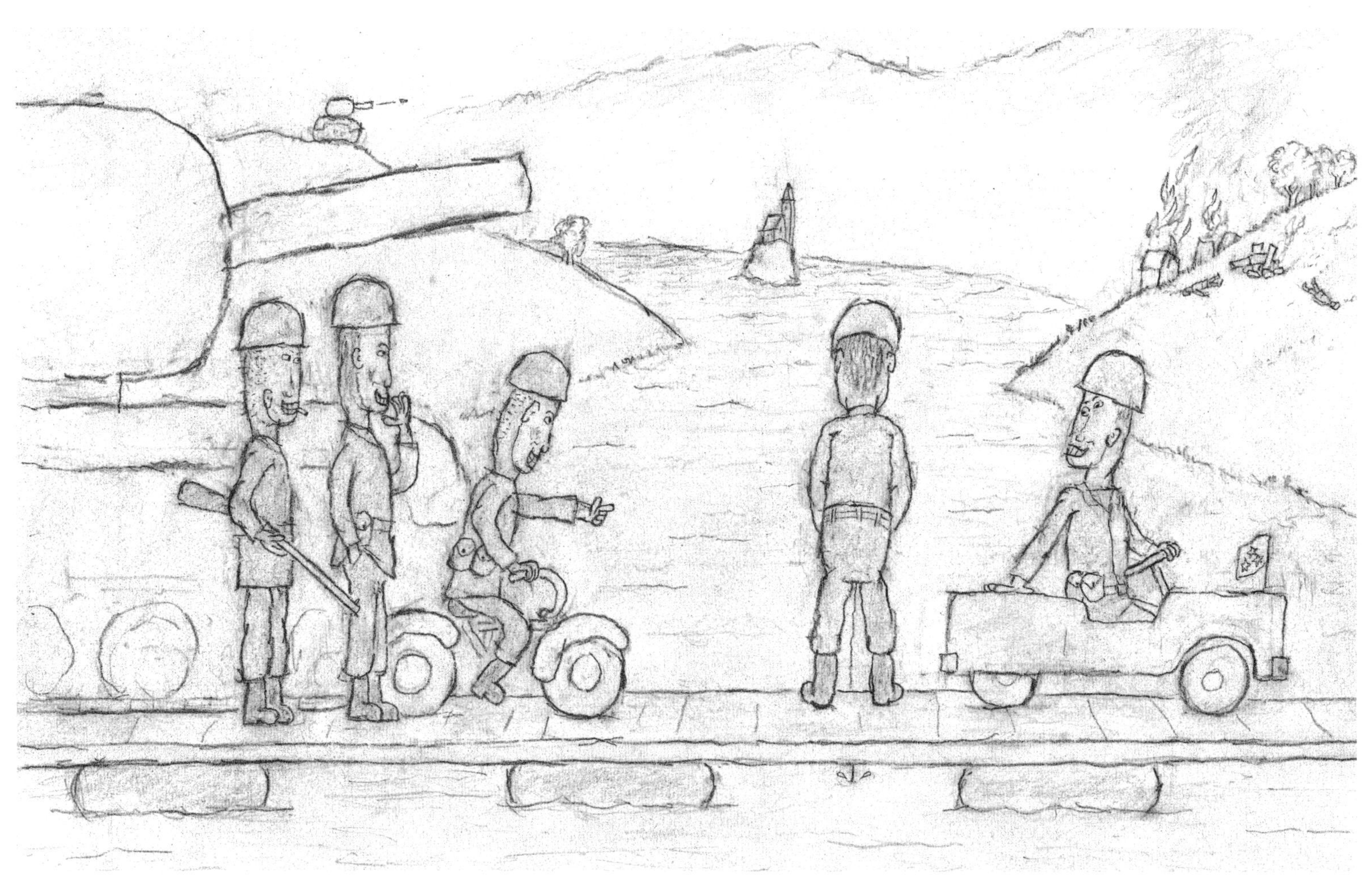

After that General Patton added insult to injury by
doing something to the Rhine River, which Hitler
said no Allied troops would ever cross over.

Then the
spaghetti eaters
fixed Il Duce.

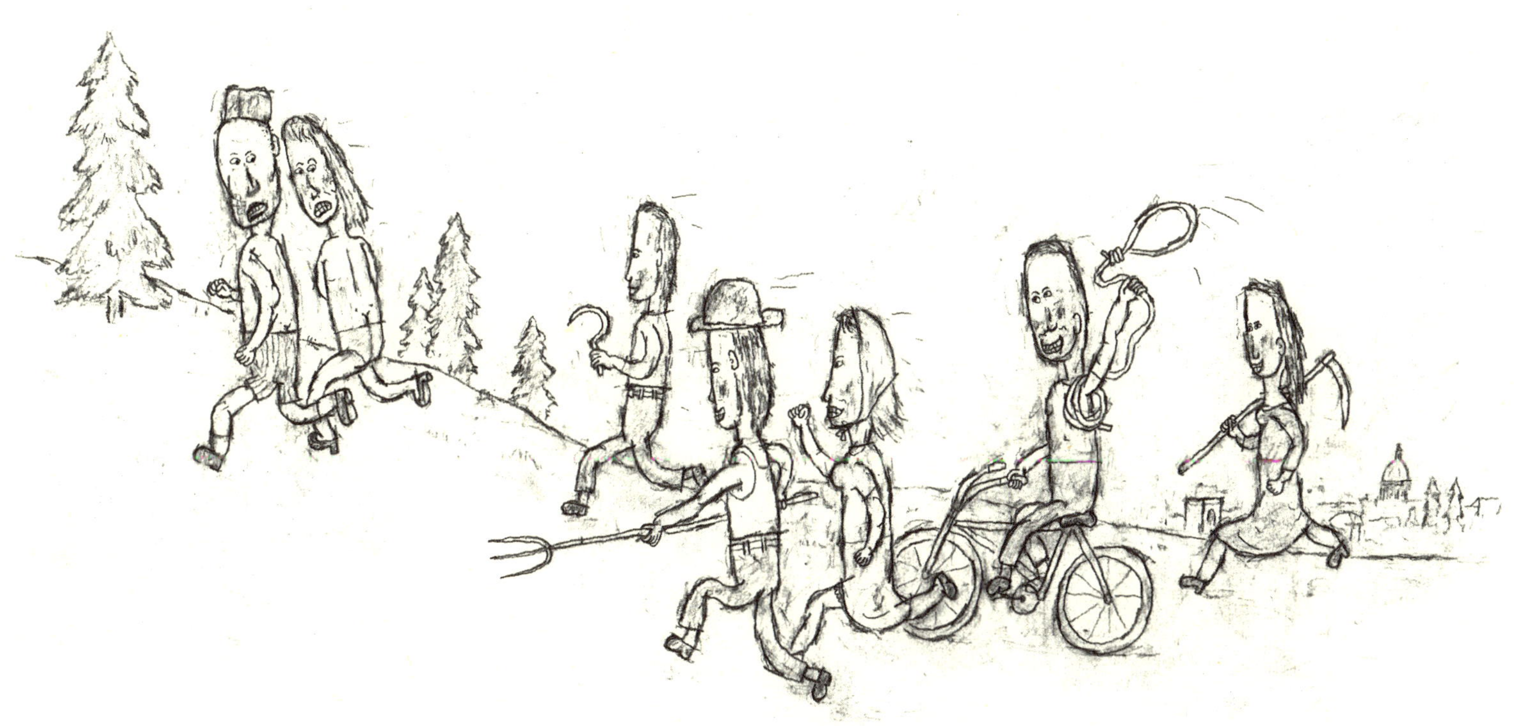

Hitler had Eva Braun go and
poison herself in their bunker.
Then Hitler poisoned and hung and
shot himself.
Then just to be sure, he burned
the bodies.

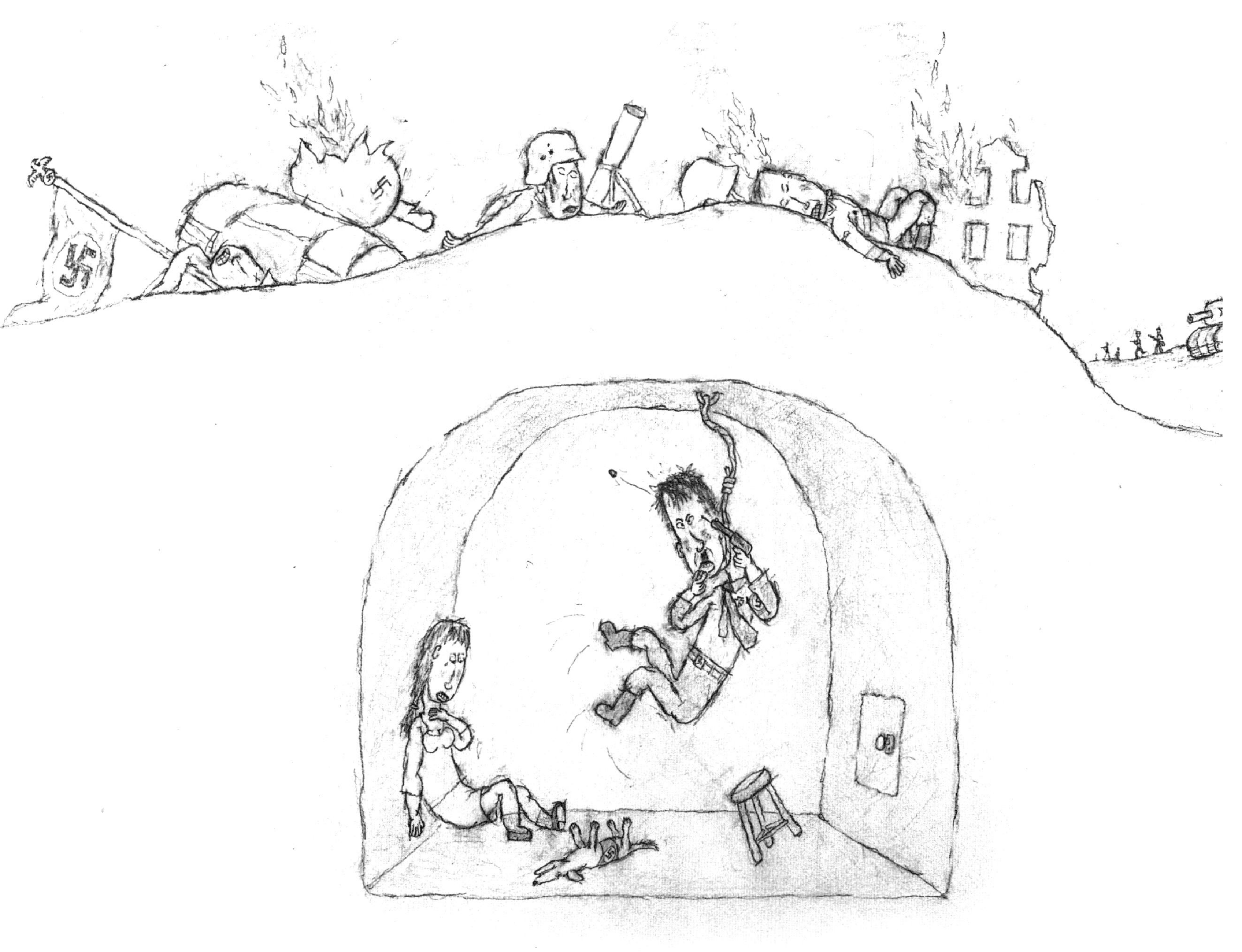

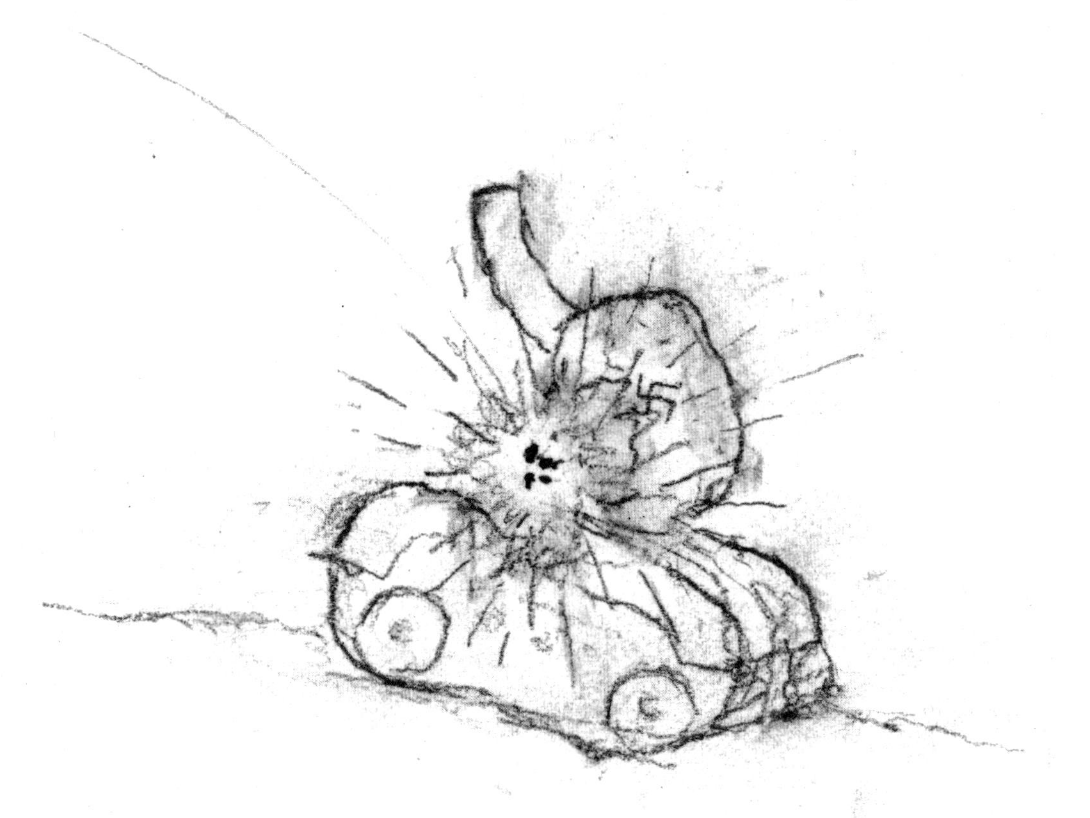

The Wehrmacht
was wiped out.

In France, here's what happened to girls who were friends with Nazis.

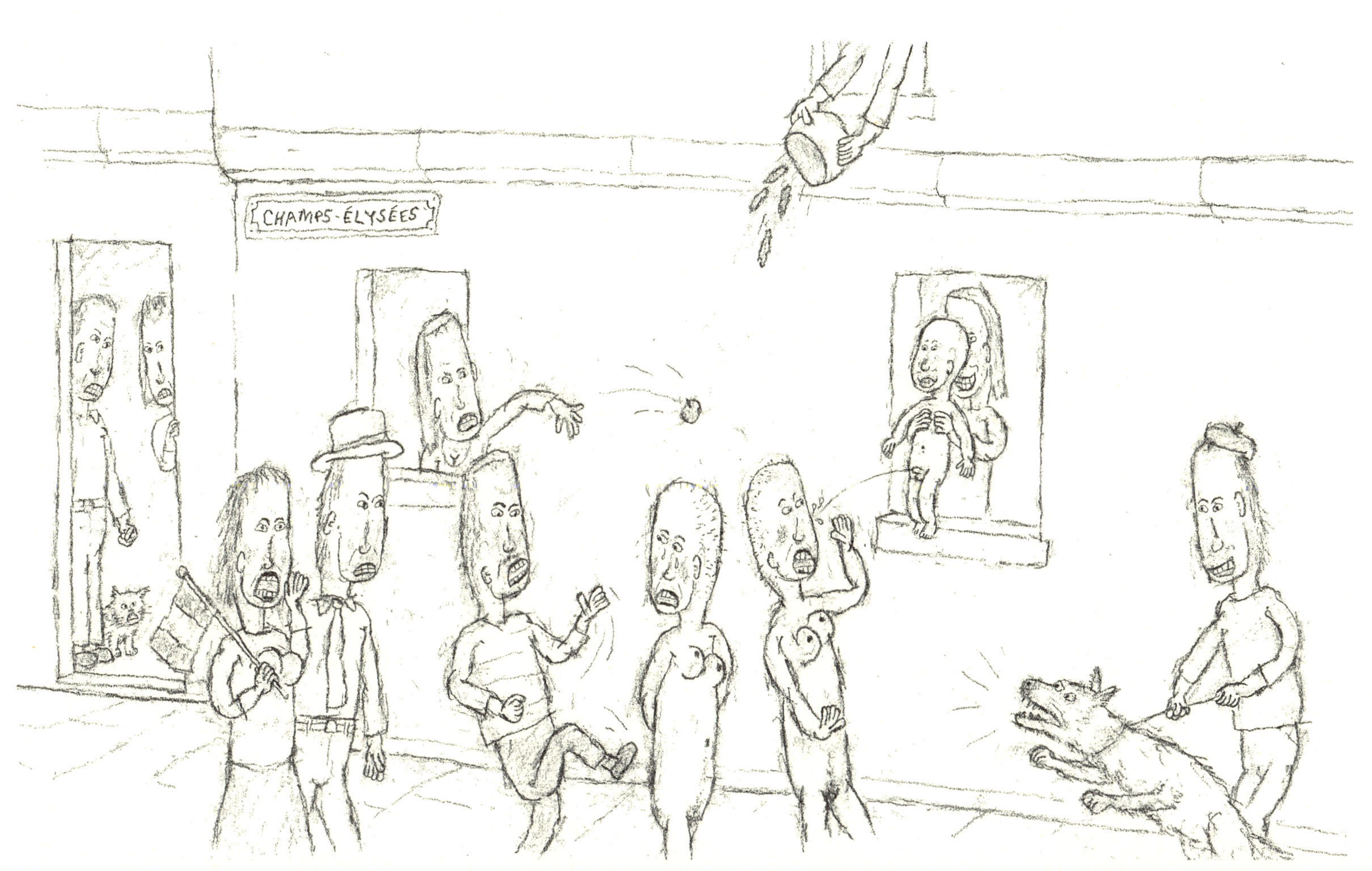

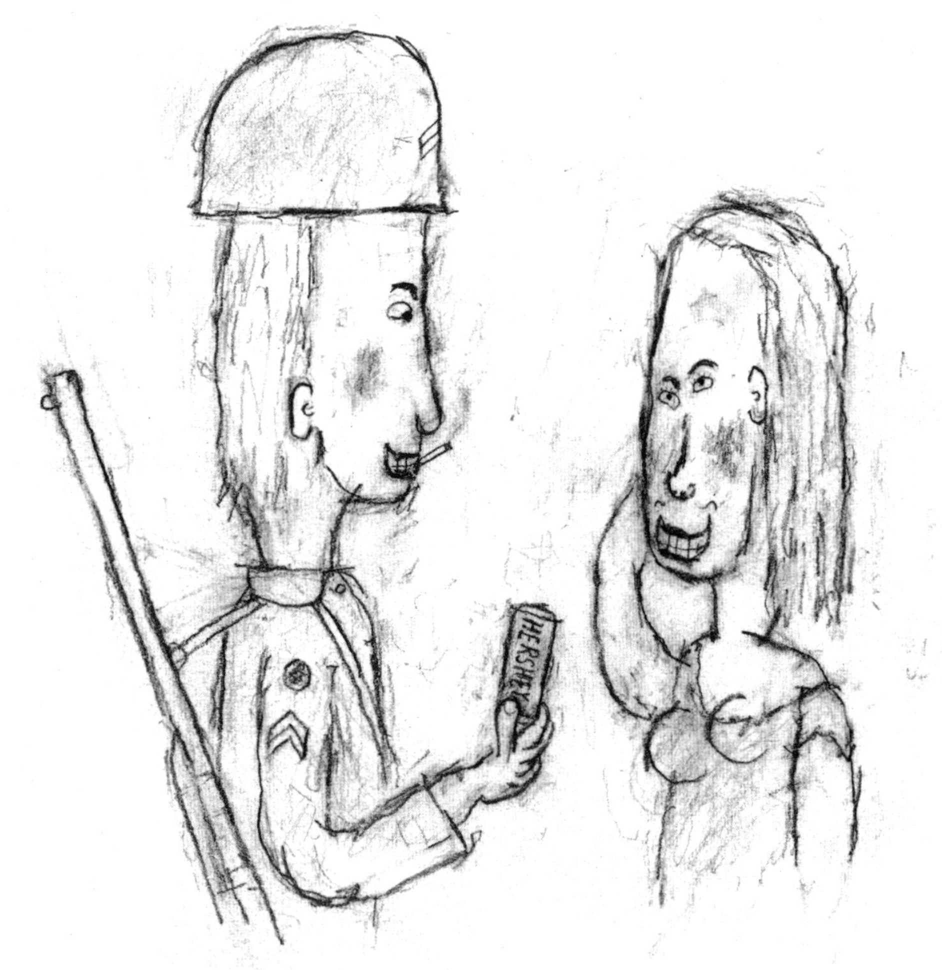

Then all the people who were left alive in Europe were kept from starving by the American GIs, who gave them chewing gum and Hershey bars (even though they were foreigners).

The fanatical Japs were
cooking up a new plan.

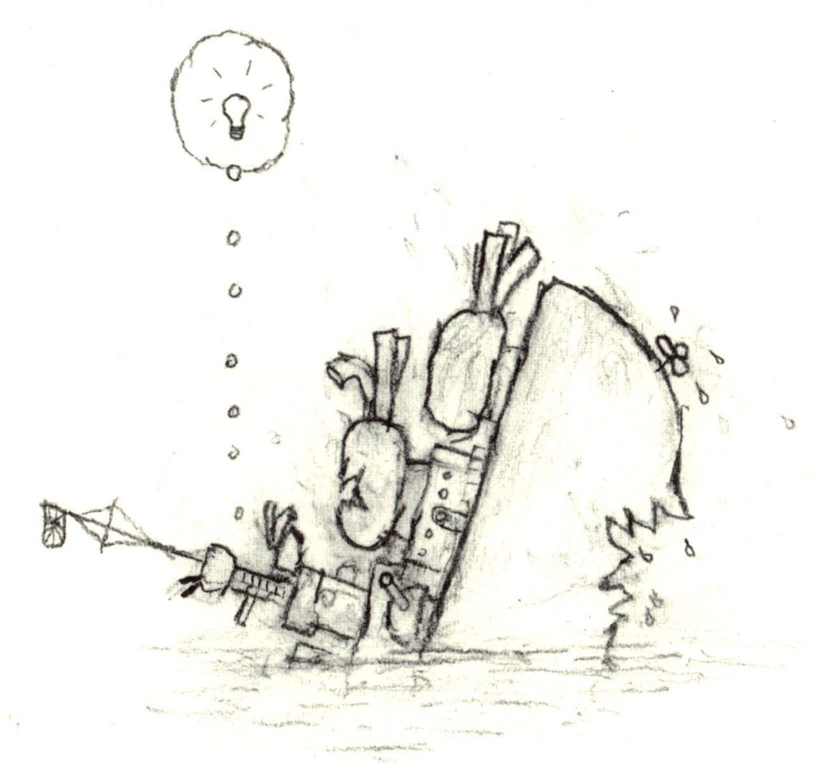

The Nip generals "asked" their
pilots to go on kamikaze missions.

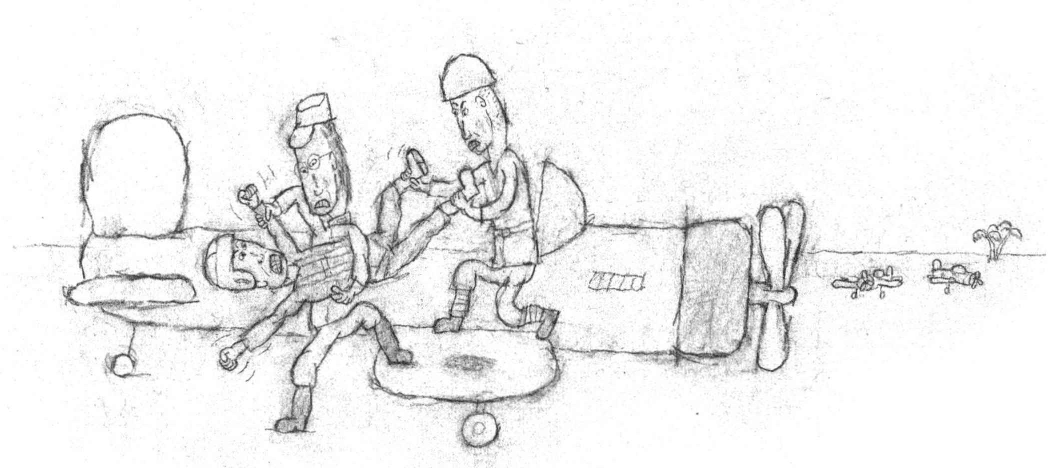

When they took off, the wheels came
off their planes, so the only place
they could land was on the U.S. Navy.

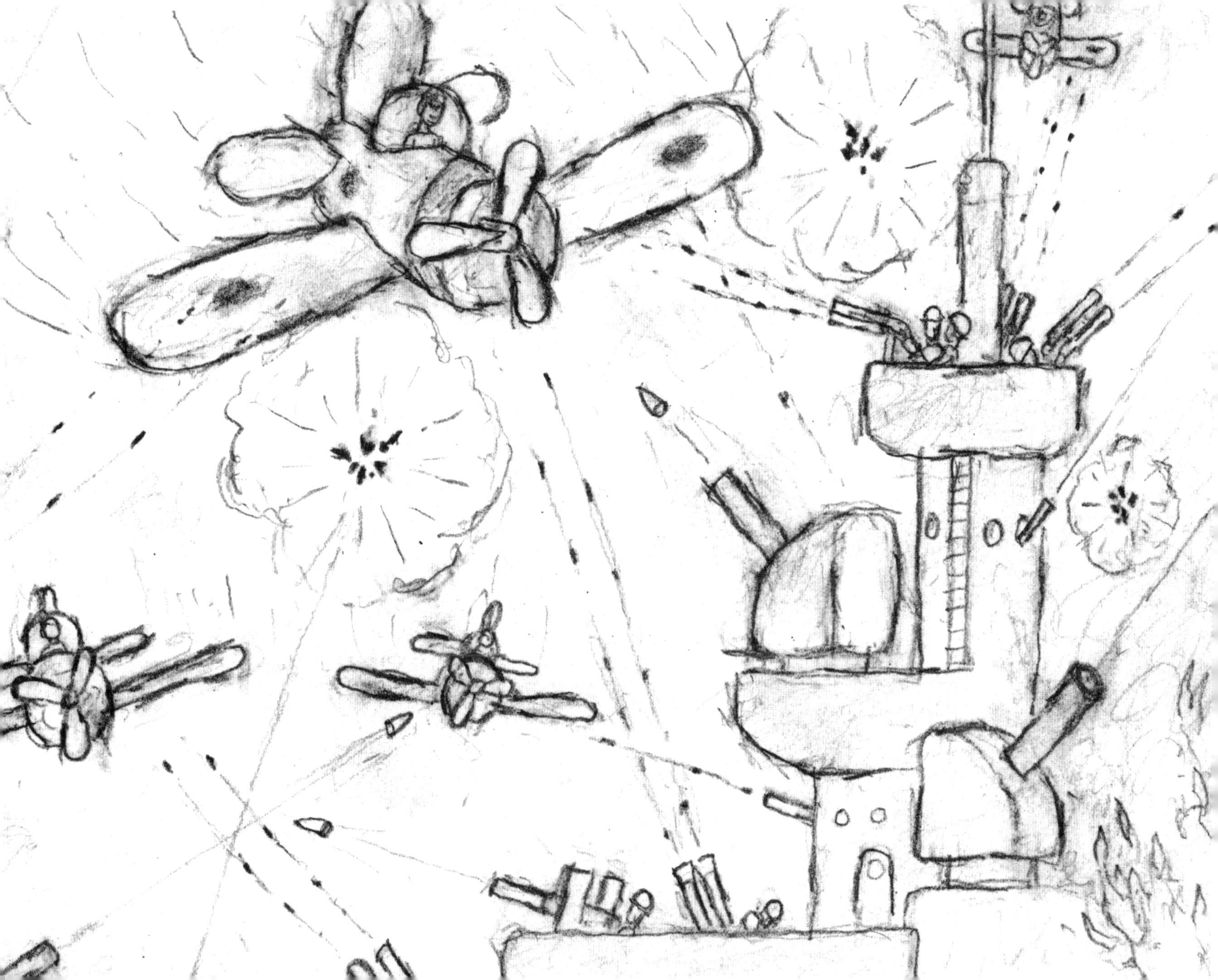

Besides taking a nosedive on American
ships, the Japs had other ways of
committing honorable hara-kiri.

Jumping off
a cliff.

Getting into a
fight with a
U.S. Marine.

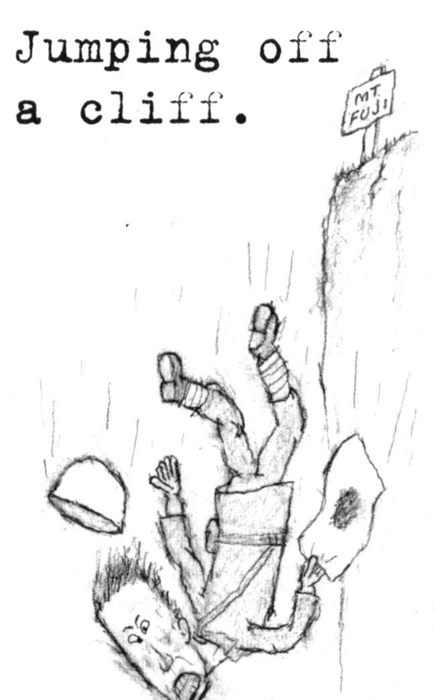

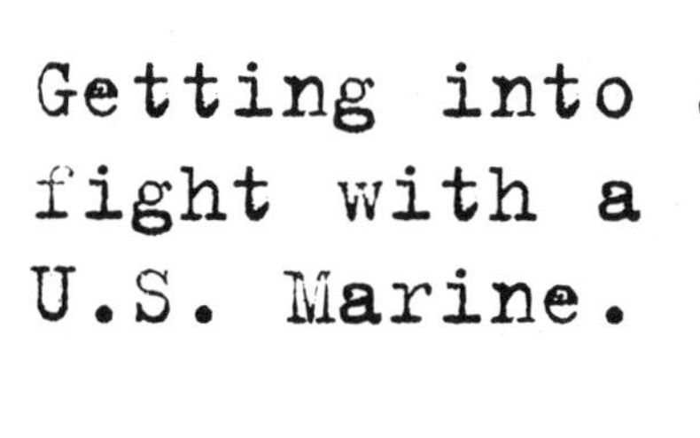

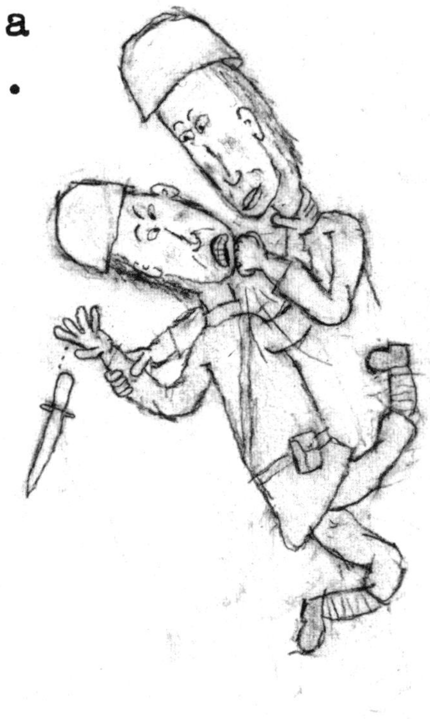

Swallowing
a grenade.

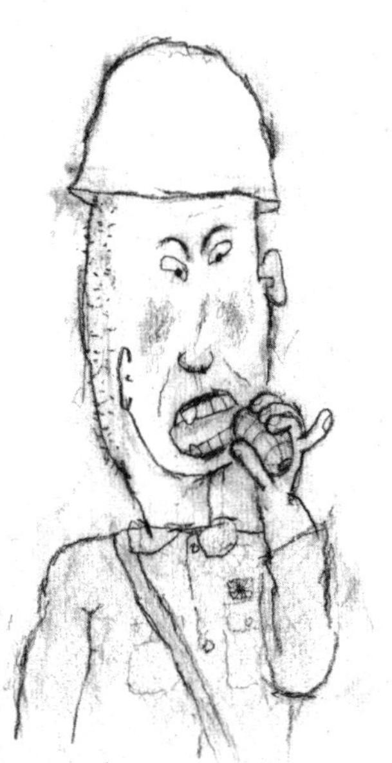

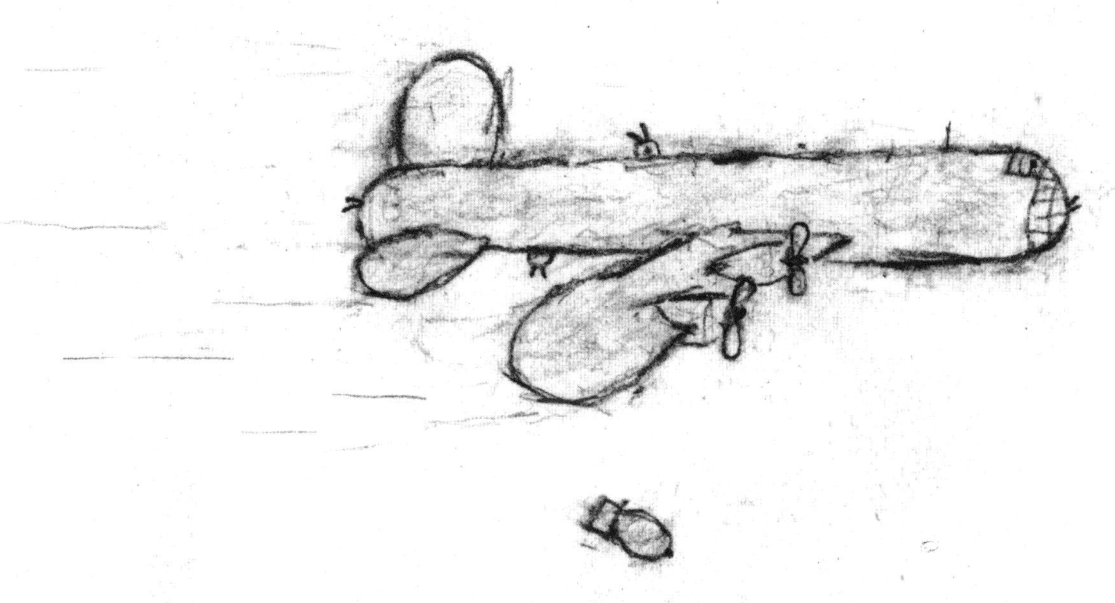

But then, with our Yankee ingenuity,
we invented a swell new bomb.

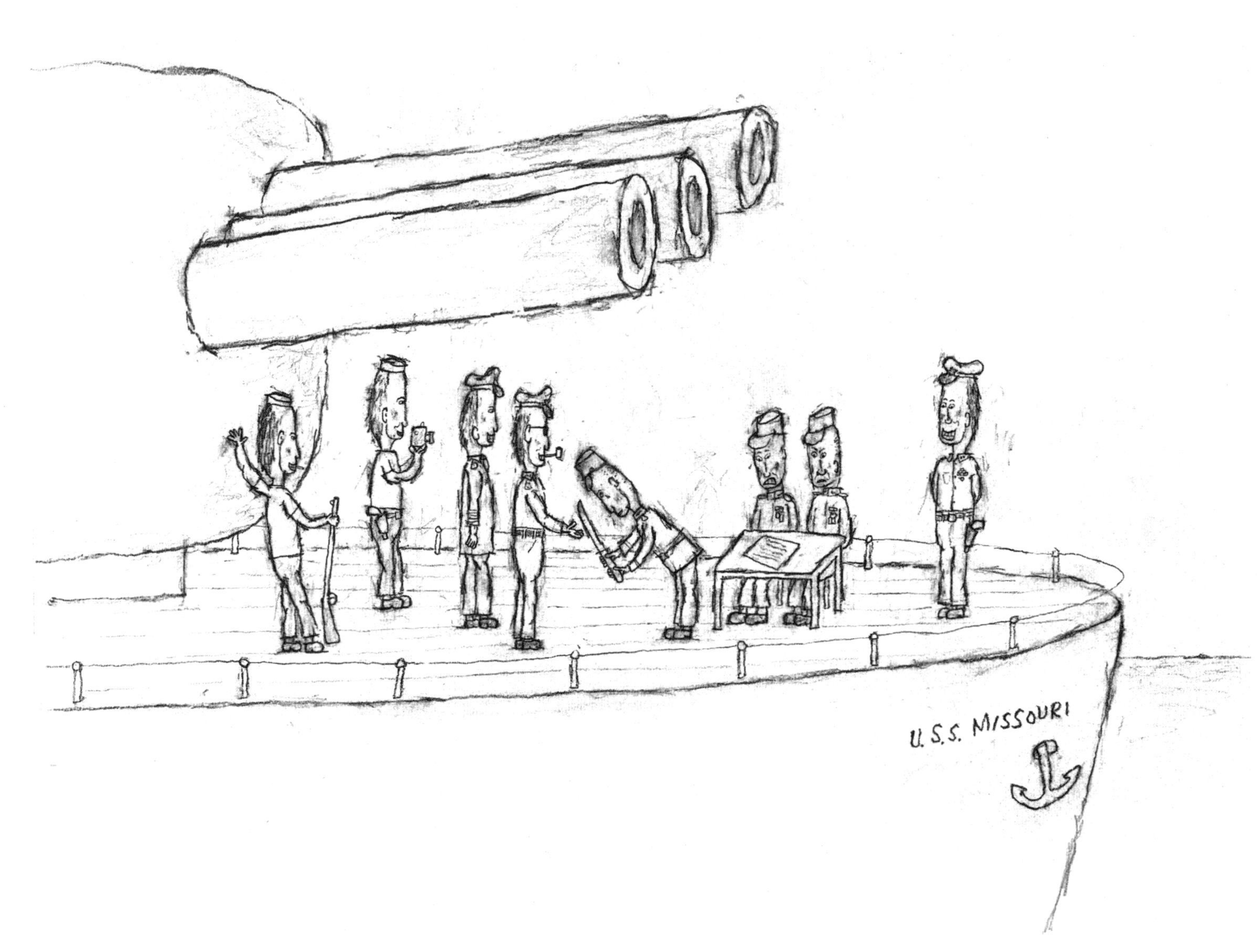

U.S.S. MISSOURI

It was curtains for Tojo
and Hitler.

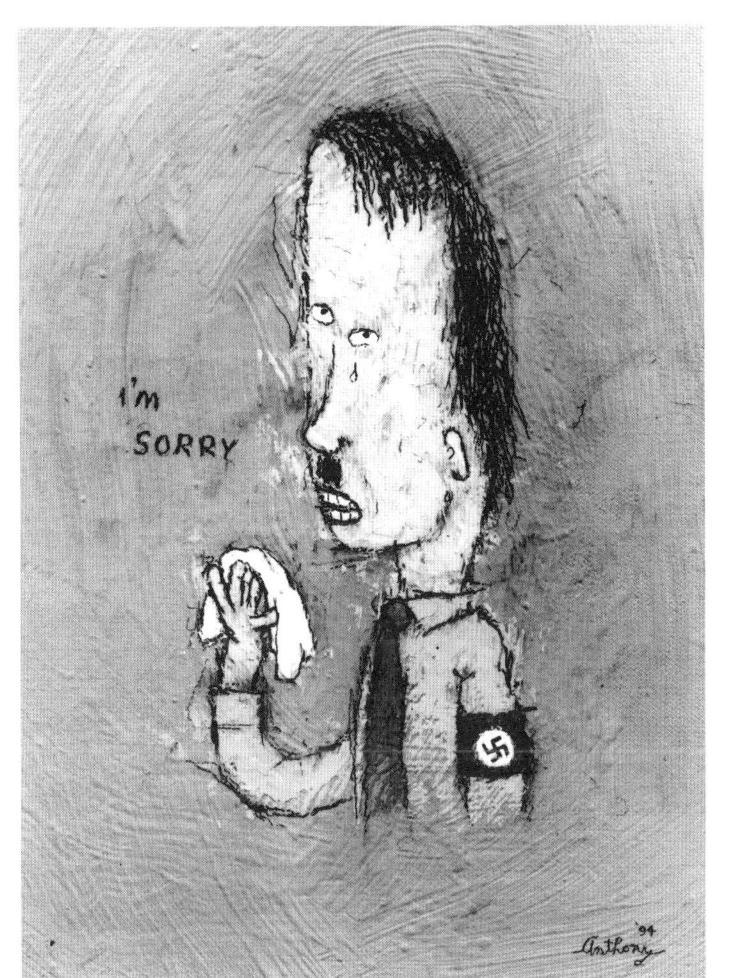

I'm
SORRY

William Anthony was born in 1934 in Fort Monmouth, New Jersey, and he grew up in Washington state. Anthony studied art briefly with Josef Albers at Yale University, where he received a B.A. degree in European history in 1958. He also studied with Theodoros Stamos at the Art Students League in New York and at a number of art schools in San Francisco. He and his wife Norma currently live in New York.

Anthony's drawings have been commissioned for Artforum, the Paris Review, Parnassus, and by Andy Warhol for his magazine Interview. The past year has seen one-man exhibitions of Anthony's paintings and drawings at Cokkie Snoei Gallery in Rotterdam, Hallway Gallery in London, and Track 16 Gallery in Santa Monica, California.

Anthony's work is represented in the following collections:
Art Institute of Chicago
Cleveland Museum of Art
Corcoran Museum of Art, Washington, D.C.
Detroit Museum of Art
Ludwig Museum, Cologne
Metropolitan Museum of Art, New York
Museum of Contemporary Art, Chicago
Museum of Fine Arts, Houston
Seattle Art Museum
Solomon R. Guggenheim Museum, New York
University Art Museum, Berkeley
Whitney Museum of American Art, New York
Yale University Art Museum, New Haven, Connecticut

As long time fans of Willam Anthony's acerbic wit, we are proud as punch that Bill has chosen Smart Art Press to publish *War Is Swell*.—TP
Acerbically speaking, you might want to sample one or more of the titles below.

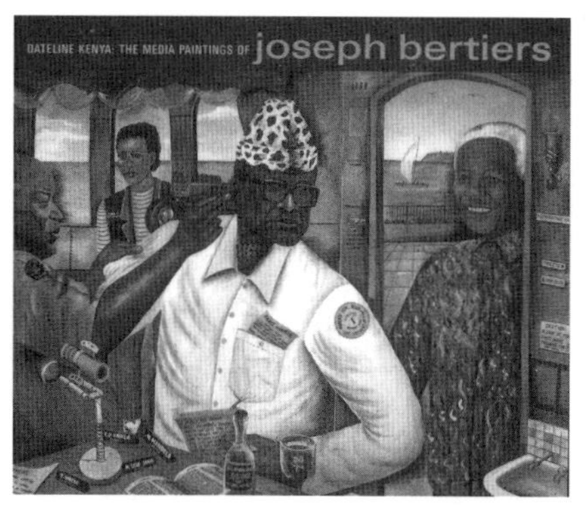

42. *Dateline Kenya: The Media Paintings of Joseph Bertiers*
Although Joseph Bertiers has never set foot outside Kenya, his addiction to current events via television, radio, newspapers, and magazines has fueled a unique style of painting that bridges the gap between "naive" art and the sociopolitical issues of the 1990s. Essay by Karal Ann Marling, interview with Bertiers by Ernie Wolfe III.
Softcover, 9¾ x 9¾ inches
72 pp
58 color and 3 black-and-white reproductions
ISBN 1-889195-20-0
$20

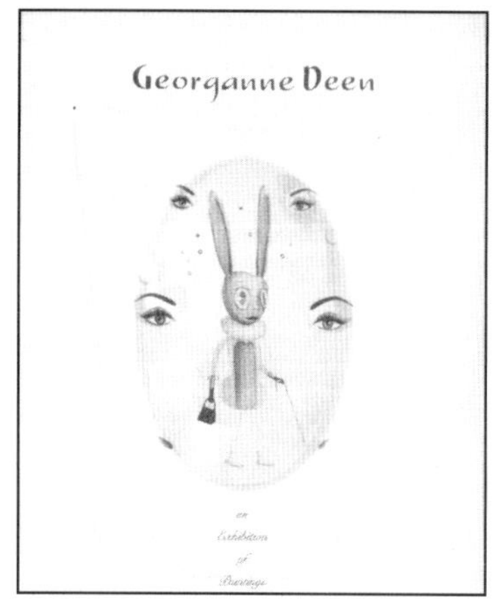

27. *Georganne Deen*
Rendered in a comic style, Georganne Deen's exquisite paintings mine emotionally charged materials and explore the dynamics of dysfunction with extraordinary honesty. Essays by Amy Gerstler and Michael Zakian.
Softcover, 9 x 7 inches
36 pp
17 color and 4 black-and-white reproductions
ISBN 1-889195-11-1
$10

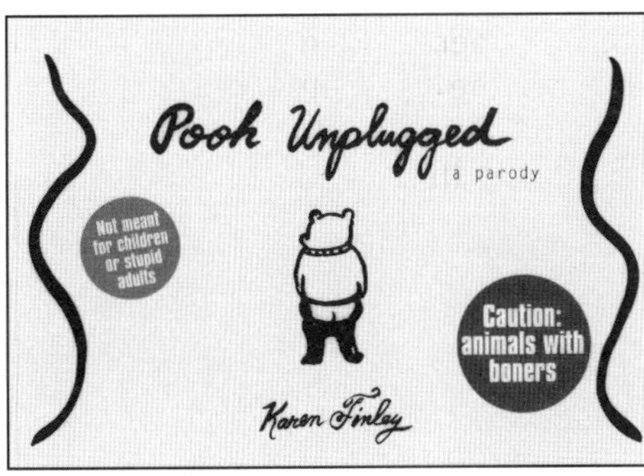

49. *Karen Finley: Pooh Unplugged, A Parody*
In the spirit of Karen Finley's riotous performances, *Pooh Unplugged* dissects social hypocrisy and commercialism by moving Pooh and Christopher Robin, Tigger and Eeyore out of their fairy tale and into real life.
Hardcover, 7 x 10 inches
64 pp
54 black-and-white reproductions
ISBN 1-889195-26-X
$19.95

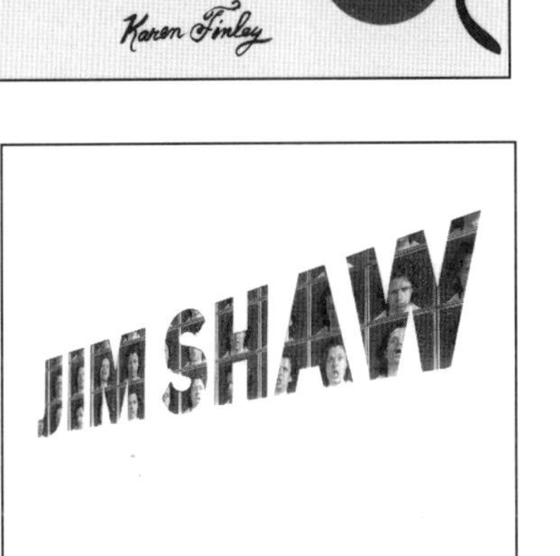

58. *Jim Shaw: Everything Must Go*
A survey of his career from 1974 to the present, *Everything Must Go* is the first catalogue to incorporate the full range of Jim Shaw's profoundly original and idiosyncratic work. Essays by Amy Gerstler, Doug Harvey, Mike Kelley, Noëllie Roussel, and Fabrice Stroun.
Softcover, 10 x 8¼ inches
150 pp
75 color and 35 black-and-white reproductions
ISBN 2-919893-23-8
$25

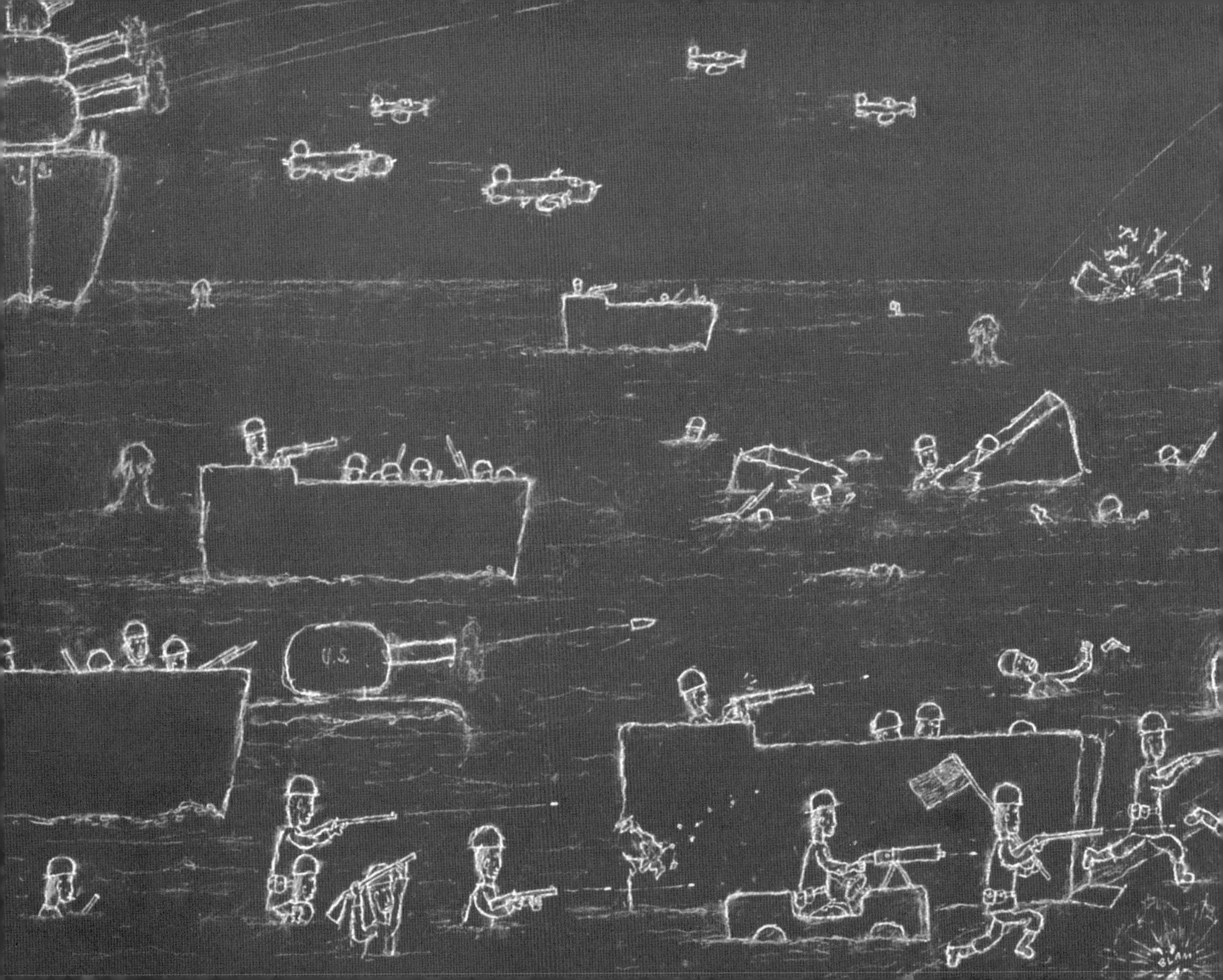
U.S.
BLAM